**SEXY, NOURISHING FOOD
TO FUEL
YOUR BODY, MIND & SOUL**

Sexy Nourishing Food to Fuel Your Mind, Body, and Soul
By Chef Amber Caudle
    Lizzie Rose Reiss, Co-Author

Text Copyright © 2021 by Amber Caudle and Lizzie Rose Reiss
Photography Copyright © 2021 by Hailee Repko and Jake Repko, CNW
Layout, Cover, and Design: Stacie Martinez, The Lucky Bandana
Food Styling, Art Direction: Hailee Repko, CNW

Published by Legacy Press Books
311 Main St., Suite D
El Segundo, CA 90245
Published and Printed in the United States of America

ISBN: 978-1-950326-89-1

All information and recipes presented and written within, *Sexy Nourishing Food to Fuel Your Mind, Body, and Soul*, are intended for informational purposes only. You should not rely on this information as a substitute for, nor does it replace, professional medical advice, diagnosis, or treatment. If you have any concerns or questions about your health, you should always consult with a physician or other health-care professional.

grandma & me

This book is dedicated to my Grandma, who was my first teacher in the kitchen.

Sexy Nourishing Food

TO FUEL YOUR
BODY, MIND & SOUL

AMBER CAUDLE
AND LIZZIE ROSE REISS

table of contents

Introduction **9**

My Story **10**

How to Use This Book **10**

Ingredient and Dietary Notes **11**

Essential Equipment & Ingredients **12**

Adaptogens **13**

Activating Nuts and Seeds **13**

Milks, Tonics & Elixirs **14**

Smoothies and Bowls **22**

Breakfast **33**

Breads **45**

Soups **52**

Salads **61**

Veggie Mains & Sides **68**

Bison & Fish **80**

Snacks & Sweets **92**

Aiolis, Pestos & Dips **105**

What I Love About Superfoods **110**

Acknowledgements **112**

introduction

I always feel my sexiest, happiest, and strongest when I'm nourishing my body with delicious whole foods that combine provocative flavor with superb nutrition. Call me kitchen kinky, but I get turned on by how food can heal me. What I mean is this: beautiful foods from the earth have this inherent wisdom, the power to nourish and heal, and they can stimulate both excitement from your taste buds and healthy, happy functioning of your vital organs and bodily functions. I cannot think of anything that makes me happier than that.

I have had a love affair with food my whole life. At times it was *innocent*, full of love and care, like when I started baking in the kitchen with my Grandma. At times it's been *turbulent*, as I relied on binging or restricting to give me a sense of control. Sometimes it's been straight up *unhealthy*, as I relied on sugar to make me feel comforted at times when I needed to do deep healing. It's been *inspiring* to learn under or work with chefs I admire. It's been *stimulating* to navigate the creative journey of developing recipes that live up to my high standards of both flavor and function. What is love, if not a journey of discovery and growth? I feel it all with food, and I want to share my love affair with you.

I've discovered that my purpose in life is to inspire people through food; to share how good we can feel when we're putting the right foods into our bodies. (And the *right* foods are different for everyone. What gets me going might not work for you.)

So many people believe healthy food is bland. But it doesn't have to be that way. Healthy is the new sexy! We don't need to feel deprived when we are taking care of our bodies. We need to eat and enjoy our food, let it nourish and excite us.

It's not all about taking care of the future-you. What we put into our bodies makes a difference now. So many people walk around foggy-brained, bloated, inflamed, fatigued, gassy, uncomfortable. And many don't even notice it anymore. What if you could walk around feeling energized, alive, and clear? It takes some trial and error to figure out what works for you, but choosing the right foods for your unique body has the power to change your life.

my story

In 2009 I hit my "rock bottom" when I had to have surgery on my hip as a result of the way I had been treating my body. I realized I had been abusing food my whole life. I had an addictive relationship with sugar, I was overeating, and I wasn't treating food or my body with the respect they both deserve. Once I fully realized what I had been doing, I was determined to feel better and rid my body of unnecessary inflammation, bloating, weight, and brain fog. I wanted to feel happy and free in my body and I did not want to feel deprived. I became inspired and unstoppable. This became a purpose-driven spiritual journey for me as I opened The Source Cafe in 2012 and started my true work in the world. I want to make a paradigm shift in our world through food, and I feel I get to work towards that goal every day at my restaurants and with this book. Thank you so much for joining me on the journey.

how to use this book

I used to have food rules. But what good are rules when you always want to break them? Instead of food rules, I honor food choices. I have a policy about listening to my body. I listen to what she wants that will nourish her, what she wants that might harm her, how she feels when holding or thinking about a particular food, and how she feels once she's eaten it. I notice when I feel strength or energy, physically or mentally. I aim for presence with my body around food, and I encourage you to do the same.

Take your time when you're choosing your foods and when you're eating them. One moment of pausing to remember mindful food practices won't make a difference in your schedule, but it will make a difference in your body.

The recipes in this book are carefully crafted to suit my needs and desires for optimal health and vitality. Some things that work for me might not serve you. I encourage you to try substituting foods that excite you. Do your research to find out about the nutritional properties of different foods you love and hate. Try things you've never tried before and notice how your body responds. I want this book to be a support and a guide for you as you navigate your own journey with healthy eating.

ingredient & dietary notes

I get asked all the time about which diet I follow, or which foods I love and hate. I am super choosy about the foods I put in my body, but I don't follow any specific diet. I listen to my body. While I don't have specific food rules, my experience listening to my body has led me to these guidelines.

Meat as an accompaniment to a plant-full plate. My plate is mostly full of veggies before I add meat to the party. I choose my meats carefully, preferring sustainable wild fish and grass-fed wild bison. Eating the colors of the rainbow through whole foods from the earth can provide us with all the vitamins, minerals, and nutrients we need.

Avoid processed foods as much as possible. The labels can be so sneaky! Even the healthy-looking packaged foods can contain non-food ingredients I just don't want in my body.

Organic and non-GMO for the win. Quality of ingredients matters! I always use organic nuts and seeds, organic berries, and organic wines. I use organic fruits and veggies or find produce from a local farm whose practices I'm comfortable with. (The USDA certified organic label is very expensive... if you find a local farm that hasn't invested in the label, but uses good practices, that's a great option.) Conventional berries and nuts are directly sprayed with several chemicals, some of which are proven to cause cancer. Do your research. Choose clean.

Clean oils. I don't use canola oil or vegetable oil. They're highly processed, usually chemically processed, and when used at a high heat, the molecular structure is altered and it leads to the formation of trans-fats. The crops used to make the oil are often GMO. And these oils are high in omega-6 fatty acids that promote inflammation. Instead, I choose olive oil, coconut oil, or avocado oil.

No more gluten. It took me a long time to determine that gluten was causing problems for me. I'm so glad I've found other ways to make beautiful breads because I just can't have gluten anymore. This book is completely gluten-free, and still has lots of delicious bread.

Stay away from refined sugar. Instead, I use maple syrup, raw honey, coconut sugar, lucuma, or monk fruit. Refined sugar causes inflammation in my body. It can lead to diabetes, brain fog, an exhausted nervous system, and can negatively impact my adrenal function and my sleep. And for me, it's addictive. Who needs it? (Especially when substitutes are available!)

Stay away from dairy. Will I taste a special cheese from time to time? You bet! But in my everyday diet, I don't use dairy at all. It gives me brain fog, constipation, and I don't see any health benefits coming from dairy.

Prioritize elimination. I make proper digestion and elimination my number one priority. If I'm not pooping regularly, then I'm not happy or comfortable. It's important to keep things moving. Foods with good fiber help. You'll see a lot of references to elimination in this book. Let's get comfortable talking about poop!

essential equipment & ingredients

PANTRY STAPLES

- high-quality extra virgin olive oil
- coconut oil and/or avocado oil
- pink Himalayan sea salt
- activated pumpkin seeds (I use the Raw brand)
- quinoa
- brown rice
- organic free-range eggs
- chlorella powder
- maca powder
- lion's mane mushroom powder
- granulated monk fruit sweetener and monk fruit powder
- collagen powder
- vanilla pea protein powder (I use Nuzest)
- almond milk and/or seed milk
- gluten-free flour blend (I use Bob's Red Mill All-Purpose)
- coconut butter (I use Artisana)
- coconut milk (I use full-fat coconut milk from the can)

PRODUCE

- frozen veggie pieces for smoothies (cauliflower, sweet potato, broccoli, zucchini)
- carrots
- lettuce
- cilantro
- parsley
- butternut squash
- cauliflower
- wild or organic blueberries
- avocados

PROTEIN

- wild grass-fed bison (I use Wild Idea Buffalo)
- wild cod and/or salmon
- wild sardines

EQUIPMENT

- high-speed blender with a tamper (I love my Vitamix!)
- A good chef's knife (not too heavy in your hand.)
- food processor
- nut bag
- cast iron pan
- ceramic pot with lid (I use Le Creuset)

LEGEND

- (v) Vegan
- (p) Paleo
- (nf) Nut-free
- (k) Keto
- (gf) Gluten-free
- (df) Dairy-free

adaptogens

My first recommendations with adaptogens are:
1. Always check with your doctor.
2. Always start with small quantities and work your way up.

Adaptogens help the body adapt to stress and can help your body adapt to absorb nutrients and minerals with better efficacy. I'm not sure what I would do without adaptogens these days. From adaptogenic mushrooms to cacao to maca, I get so much from these little herbs! You can read more about each one on page 110.

activating nuts & seeds

I always recommend using activated nuts and seeds because you will receive more nutrients from them and you will digest them more easily. But if you don't have time, you can still get a lot from an un-activated nut or seed. ("Sprouted" means the same thing as "activated" in this context. A sprouted seed is an activated seed, and vice-versa.)

Activating a nut or seed simply means to soak and rinse it, removing the enzyme inhibitors so that the nut or seed begins the process of germination, making it both easier to digest and easier to benefit from.
Store activated nuts and seeds in the refrigerator for 2 days. Dehydrated, they can be stored dry for 2 weeks or frozen for 2 months.

To activate:
Place your nuts or seeds in a bowl or glass jar. Cover them with purified water. Be sure all the nuts or seeds are covered in water. Let them sit on the counter, uncovered, for at least 7 hours. You can leave them overnight.
In the morning, or once their first sitting is complete, strain the nuts or seeds using a strainer and discard the water. Rinse the strained nuts or seeds for 30 seconds.

milks,
tonics
& elixirs

NUT & SEED MILKS

Once I started making my own milks instead of buying them at the store, I never turned back. Processed milks tend to have fillers and not much of the actual nut or seed, meaning they don't have a lot of nutrition. When I make my own milks, I know exactly what I'm putting into my body. I can use great quality, clean, organic ingredients to fuel me properly. These milks are a great source of plant protein, healthy fats, and omega 3 fatty acids. If you're worried about the time it takes to make your own milk, I've got some fast and easy options for you here, too.

The following recipes are my favorites, but it's easy to get creative with what goes into your milk. You can always substitute other nuts or seeds, add some raw cacao powder for chocolate milk or cinnamon and dates for sweeter milk. Try adaptogens like maca, ashwagandha and mushroom powder for a healing milk. Consult the adaptogen information on page 13.

These milks are for smoothies, coffee or tea, granola, or just for drinking. Give a jar of milk and some homemade buckwheat granola (p. 36) for a sweet holiday gift for a health-conscious friend.

NUT & SEED MILK TIPS

NUT MILK VS. SEED MILK

I started with only nut milks, but seeds offer different omega-3 fatty acids and health benefits than nuts do. Switching to seed milks sometimes varies the nutrients I'm getting from one day to another. Since the seed milks in this book don't require straining, they're also a time-saving option.

TO SWEETEN YOUR MILKS

try using honey, dates, or maple syrup. I recommend 4 dates or 2 tablespoons of honey or maple syrup for a full batch of milk. To sweeten without sugar, try a few drops of stevia or 2 tablespoons of granulated monk fruit sweetener. Of course, more or less is just fine. Blend the sweetener into your milk little by little to get the flavor you're looking for.

ACTIVATING NUTS & SEEDS

helps our bodies access and absorb all the nutrients they have to offer. If you don't have time to activate your nuts (p. 13), don't worry. They're still good for you. Activating them just lets you absorb the most nutrition out of your nuts and seeds.

NUT MILKS

Each of these recipes makes about 4 cups of milk

The tri nut milk and almond date milk require straining. After blending all the ingredients, pour the mixture through a nut bag over a large bowl and squeeze the bag until you've gotten out as much milk as you can. You can keep the nut pulp if you have a use for it, or discard it. Store leftover milk in an airtight glass mason jar in the fridge for up to 4 days.

TRI-NUT MILK

Brazil Nut, Cashew, Walnut

This milk is deliciously rich thanks to the combination of these three very different nuts. At The Source Cafe, we steam this milk with maple syrup and espresso for a truly decadent latte. If you're feeling adventurous, you can try your own nut or seed combination.

½ cup activated brazil nuts
½ cup activated cashews
½ cup activated walnuts
a pinch of sea salt
3 ½ cups filtered water

After blending for 45 seconds, strain through a nut bag and enjoy.

ALMOND DATE MILK

Sweetened Almond Milk

You can add or subtract dates to adjust the sweetness of this milk to suit your taste. I just love the way the dates complement the flavor of the almonds. Make chocolate milk by adding ¼ cup raw cacao powder and 2 tablespoons of maple syrup.

1 cup activated raw almonds
4 dates, pitted
a pinch of sea salt
3 ½ cups filtered water

After blending for 45 seconds, strain through a nut bag and enjoy.

FAST NUT MILK

No-Strain Nut Milk

This is the fast and easy way to make your own nut milk. It's great in a pinch, mess- and stress-free. Choose your nut butter wisely: avoid fillers, sweeteners, and ingredients you don't recognize. Roasted nut butter will taste different than raw, so try both and see what you like best.

½ cup organic creamy almond butter, raw or roasted
a pinch of sea salt
4 cups filtered water

Blend everything together for just 20 seconds, then enjoy.

SEED MILKS

Both of these recipes make about 4 cups of milk

Blend all the ingredients together in a high-speed blender for 45 seconds. Store any leftover milk in an airtight glass mason jar in the fridge for up to 5 days.

PUMPKIN SEED CINNAMON MILK

Pumpkin seeds have a few really amazing benefits that get me excited to use them as often as I can. They contain tryptophan, the amino acid that helps you produce serotonin and melatonin, both of which promote healthy sleep. Pumpkin seeds help improve your metabolism, and they're full of omega-3 and omega-6 fatty acids, antioxidants, and fiber. Plus, they contain 12 grams of protein per cup!

½ cup activated pumpkin seeds*
2 teaspoons cinnamon
a pinch of sea salt
4 cups filtered water

HEMP SEED COCONUT MILK

Everything I learn about hemp seeds (sometimes called hemp hearts) makes me love them more. They're another unique superstar of the seed world... except they're technically nuts, not seeds. Here are some of my favorite things about hemp seeds:

- *They are a complete protein because they contain all nine essential amino acids.*
- *They are 30% fat, especially high in omega-3 and omega-6 fatty acids.*
- *Hemp seeds are much more easily digestible than other nuts, seeds, or grains.*
- *They are wonderful for your heart, your circulation, your energy, and reducing inflammation.*

¼ cup hemp seeds
¼ cup softened coconut butter**
a pinch of sea salt
4 cups filtered water

*I love the "Raw" brand because they're already activated.
**I like the brand "Artisana." You can soften it in the microwave or in a double boiler.

TONICS & ELIXIRS

The tonics and elixirs in this chapter are full of health benefits. Each one of them has a purpose. They may be somewhat unconventional, but they represent the theme of this book and my work for the last several years: **food can help you heal and thrive** (even in liquid form!) These tonics and elixirs are a helpful trick to have up your sleeve when you find yourself in need of some nutritional support.

ADAPTOGEN CACAO LATTE
(ADULT HOT CHOCOLATE)

Makes 1 serving

This latte gives me lots of clean energy while helping with my adrenal and hormonal balance. There are a lot of adaptogens in this one, so see page 13 to read about how to properly use adaptogens. I like including mushrooms, another anti-cancer superfood, which are also anti-inflammatory and help with mental clarity, longevity, and all around vitality. The maca* is great for stamina, libido, and hormone balance as well. I think of this latte as a sexy hot chocolate for adults.

1 ½ cups tri nut milk (p. 16)
2 tablespoons raw cacao powder**
1 tablespoon lucuma powder
1 tablespoon mesquite powder
1 tablespoon tocos powder
1 tablespoon maple syrup
1 teaspoon maca powder*

½ teaspoon ground cinnamon
¼ teaspoon lion's mane mushroom powder

***Optional:
½ teaspoon ashwagandha powder
¼ teaspoon reishi mushroom powder

For a hot latte, start by heating the milk in a kettle on the stove until gently boiling. Hot or cold, blend all the ingredients together for about 45 seconds in a high-speed blender. Enjoy warm or pour over ice to enjoy it cold.

*Skip the maca if you are pregnant, breastfeeding, or balancing your hormones.
**Raw Cacao can be energizing, especially if you're sensitive and/or not a regular caffeine drinker.
***I love to add all mushrooms and ashwagandha for extra nervous system support and hormone balance.

MATCHA LATTES

Each recipe makes one serving

For a hot latte, start by heating the milk in a kettle on the stove until gently boiling. Hot or cold, blend all the ingredients together for about 45 seconds in a high-speed blender. Enjoy warm or pour over ice to enjoy it cold.

SIMPLE MATCHA LATTE

When I'm looking for an energy boost, I prefer green tea to coffee. This latte is my favorite drink for getting energized without the jitters.

1 ½ cups pumpkin cinnamon milk (p. 17)
1 tablespoon softened coconut butter***
1 teaspoon matcha powder
1 teaspoon maca* powder

Optional: 2 tablespoons protein or collagen powder

BRAIN FUEL LATTE

I'm known for my weird ingredient combinations, but I've learned to trust my crazy kitchen intuition. The results are almost always delicious, and this unexpected latte is no exception. It's packed with adaptogens and healthy fats, making it great for energy, memory, cognitive function, and mental clarity.

If you're not used to eating a lot of superfoods at once, this latte can feel overwhelming for your body. Always start with small quantities of adaptogens and superfoods and work your way up.

1 ½ cups pumpkin seed cinnamon milk (p. 17)
1 tablespoon maple syrup or 2 pitted dates
1 tablespoon MCT oil**
1 tablespoon tocos powder
1 teaspoon matcha powder
1 drop rosemary essential oil (safe for internal consumption)

*Skip the maca if you're pregnant, breastfeeding, or balancing your hormones.
**If you're not used to MCT oil, start with just 1 teaspoon, or substitute melted coconut oil.
*** I use the brand "Artisana." You can soften in the microwave or over a double boiler.

MATCHA

Matcha is a supercharged, earthy-tasting green tea powder that's packed with antioxidants. Green tea is often recommended as an anti-cancer superfood, and likewise, matcha is known for its many health benefits.

Make sure you know where your matcha is coming from to ensure high quality. When it comes to matcha, you always want to choose organic, unsweetened, and stone ground. My favorite brands are Reishi and Pique.

TURMERIC TONIC

Makes 8 cups

7 ½ cups filtered water
½ cup apple cider vinegar
¾ teaspoon liquid stevia
2 drops black pepper oil
1 ½ tablespoons ground turmeric
1 teaspoon ground cinnamon
½ teaspoon ground ginger
⅛ teaspoon cayenne pepper

This is the tonic that started it all. When I was in chronic pain every day, recovering from hip surgery, I began researching anti-inflammatory foods. I thought there had to be a way to use food to heal my body. I played with the essential ingredients until this recipe emerged: a tonic I could drink daily to help alleviate my inflammation and pain. Before long, my friends and their friends were ordering gallon-jugs of Turmeric Tonic. Still one of the Source Cafe's best sellers, this tonic doesn't just fight inflammation, it boosts immune system function, helps curb appetite, increases metabolism, helps lower blood pressure and cholesterol, and provides a nice energy boost. It also makes a great cure for a pesky hangover. I hope it gives you even a little bit of the support it has given me.

To maintain my health, I drink 8 ounces daily. If I feel my immune function is compromised or needs a boost, or I'm healing, I drink 16 ounces daily.

Whisk together all the ingredients and store in a glass jar in the refrigerator for up to one week.

TURMERIC LATTE

Makes 1 serving

1 ½ cups almond milk
1 tablespoon maple syrup or
honey or a few drops of stevia
1 drop black pepper essential oil or
a pinch of ground black pepper
1 teaspoon ground turmeric
½ teaspoon ground cinnamon
¼ teaspoon ground ginger

When I'm looking for something warm and comforting without caffeine, the turmeric latte is my go-to drink. I use it to help my body reset on a no-caffeine week, or as a pick-me-up in the middle of the day.

For a hot latte, start by heating the milk in a kettle on the stove until gently boiling. Hot or cold, blend all the ingredients together for about 45 seconds in a high-speed blender. Enjoy warm or pour over ice to enjoy cold.

TURMERIC

Turmeric is a powerful anti-inflammatory food that I use as often as I can, but it needs to be accompanied by black pepper to be properly absorbed into our bodies. I often use black pepper essential oil, but you can also use a pinch of ground black pepper. Turmeric without the black pepper doesn't have nearly the same benefits, so don't forget your pepper!

smoothies
& bowls

My deep love for smoothies and smoothie bowls is real, and having one is always my favorite part of the day. They're an efficient way to pack a lot of nutrition into one convenient meal, and the way I make them is a great way to get veggies into your breakfast.

I love that smoothie bowls are great for breakfast, but also work as dessert or a nutrient-dense base for granola. You can sneak veggies into these bowls and kids or picky eaters would never guess they're eating something healthy. It's a special kind of satisfaction for me to see someone who wouldn't touch cauliflower on their own ravenously enjoy a bowl that's full of it!

Using veggies instead of fruit is what makes so many of these smoothies and bowls special. You can always play around with different vegetables. Just keep the quantities the same, and you can substitute any of your favorites. Try delicata or butternut squash, broccoli, cucumber, or whatever's in season. The options are endless.

In the following pages, you'll find a few tips that make these smoothies and bowls easy to master.

BLENDERS

*For these smoothies and bowls, a high-speed blender is absolutely essential. I use a Vitamix and it's my favorite and most-used tool in the kitchen. But what you really need for these recipes is a **high-speed blender that has a tamper**. Any brand will do.*

CONSISTENCY

Blend the smoothies and bowls to your desired consistency by adding more or less of the recipe's liquid. I like a thick smoothie bowl, but if you prefer a soft-serve ice cream consistency, it requires more liquid.

MILKS

In all of these smoothies and bowls, you can use whatever milk you have on hand in place of the milk listed in the ingredients. You can even use water in a pinch if you don't mind missing a little of the richness the milks offer. Check the milk recipes on p. 16 to see which ones you might be able to throw together quickly.

NUT BUTTERS

Feel free to switch almond butter for another nut or seed butter. Try tahini! You can also substitute a quarter of a peeled and pitted avocado.

SUPERFOODS & ADAPTOGENS

If your kitchen isn't stocked with tocos, mesquite, maca, lucuma, and dulse, don't worry. You don't have to spend a fortune stocking up. Take a look at the superfood glossary on page 110 and assess what's essential for you, and what you can easily skip.

PROTEIN POWDERS

Choosing a protein powder can be tricky. I encourage you to make the choices that feel best to you. You can use your favorite one in any of these recipes. The one I use is slightly sweetened and naturally vanilla-flavored. So if you're using an unflavored protein powder, you might need to make some adjustments to keep the flavor of the smoothie at its best, like adding a little sweetness, and/or some vanilla extract. Try stevia or monk fruit powder if you want to sweeten without sugar.

Protein powder labels can be really clever, making us feel like we're eating something clean while sneaking undesirable ingredients into the product.

My rules of thumb are: **the fewer ingredients the better, don't eat anything I can't pronounce, listen to how my body feels when I eat it.** I have researched hundreds of protein powders and tried so many I can't count. The protein I use and recommend the most is Nuzest Vanilla Pea Protein, which is delicious, sugar-free, vegan, non-GMO, has only 3 ingredients, no fillers, and most importantly, it doesn't bloat me. (It's called Clean Lean Protein.) The recipes in this book have been formulated using Nuzest Vanilla Protein.

FROZEN VEGGIES

The frozen veggies are what make these bowls special. No matter how many times I explain this concept,

I still get questions about it all the time. You're essentially making "veggie ice cubes." They keep your smoothie or bowl cold without watering it down, and they add a great creamy texture along with lots of nutrients. Some veggies bring flavor, like yams, while cauliflower is hard to detect. Here's how you do it:

1. Ahead of time, cook the veggies however you want to cook them. (Roasted, steamed, etc).
2. Once the veggies are cool, place small portions in freezer bags, and lay them flat to freeze in the freezer.
3. Use the frozen cooked veggies in your smoothie for an amazing creamy texture.

GUIDE TO FROZEN FRUITS & VEGGIES

Banana: Peel ripe bananas, break in half, and freeze halves in a sealed plastic bag.

Berries: Buy wild or organic frozen berries.

Cauliflower: Steam cauliflower florets for 8-10 minutes. When cool, portion the florets into bags and freeze flat. Alternate method: Buy frozen cauliflower florets or riced

cauliflower. They're frozen raw. Use them that way, or steam first and then refreeze them. I always steam mine because I digest cauliflower better when it's been cooked.

Zucchini: Cut into quarter-sized pieces and freeze raw.

Sweet Potatoes or Yams: Roast the whole potato in a 375-degree oven for 45 minutes. When cool, peel by pulling the skin away with your fingers or a small knife, and then cut into 1-inch pieces, place in a bag and freeze flat.

Beets: Peel the beets, then chop into 1-inch cubes, and freeze raw, or steam or roast before freezing.

Carrots: Peel, slice them, and freeze raw.

Butternut Squash: Buy the frozen cubed organic squash, which is raw. Or you can peel and cube your own. You can roast before freezing it for a creamier bowl, but using it raw works just fine and is much faster.

FAVORITE GREEN SMOOTHIE

Makes one 18-ounce smoothie

1 cup filtered water or coconut water
¼ medium avocado, peeled and pitted
1 tablespoon softened coconut butter*
12 parsley leaves
12 cilantro leaves
10 mint leaves
2-3 ice cubes

Roughly Chop:
½ cup (tightly packed) dandelion greens
½ cup (tightly packed) red leaf lettuce
½ cucumber
¼ cup celery
¼ medium green apple, cored
½-inch piece of ginger root, peeled

I use the brand "Artisana." You can soften in the microwave or over a double boiler.

I'm a big fan of a green drink for a meal or a snack because it always gives me a natural energy boost. This smoothie has 10 different vegetables, fruits, and herbs, so it's full of fiber and vitamins. The ginger and mint brighten up the flavor while the coconut butter and avocado add a creamy texture that makes this super green-tasting smoothie easy to enjoy. It's not a sweet one, but I think you're going to love it.

Combine all of the ingredients in a high-speed blender with a tamper and blend until smooth, scraping down the sides as you go. Add more liquid as needed to create the consistency you're looking for.

REFUELER YAM SMOOTHIE

Makes one 18-ounce smoothie

1 ½ cups coconut water
½ cup frozen roasted yams
4 activated brazil nuts
2 tablespoons vanilla pea protein powder
1 tablespoon MCT oil**
½ teaspoon ground cinnamon

Toppings:
¼ cup unsweetened shredded coconut
1 tablespoon cacao nibs
1 tablespoon hemp seeds or sunflower seeds

**If you're not used to MCT oil, start with just 1 teaspoon, or substitute melted coconut oil.*

When I realized I could replace the bananas in my smoothies with yams, I never looked back. Yams satisfy my sweet tooth while being a relatively low-glycemic food that's high in fiber, helping me stay full longer. I call this the Refueler because every ingredient helps to re-energize and replenish my body after a workout. Sometimes I make this smoothie drinkable through a straw, and sometimes I keep it thick and eat it with a spoon with hemp or sunflower seeds sprinkled on top.

Combine all of the ingredients in a high-speed blender. Blend until smooth using a tamper, scraping down the sides as needed. Add more coconut water as needed to create the consistency you're looking for.

SOURCE CAFE SMOOTHIES

Each recipe makes a 16 ounce smoothie

For each of these recipes, combine all of the ingredients in a high-speed blender and blend until smooth, scraping down the sides as you go. Add more liquid as needed to create the consistency you're looking for.

BANANZA

On the menu at The Source Cafe since opening day, the Bananza has been a great introductory smoothie for someone who is nervous about replacing breakfast with a smoothie. Delicious and filling, it tastes like a treat, but the chia seeds, almond butter, and banana provide its nutrition. Add a scoop of protein powder for a more filling smoothie.

1 ½ cups hemp seed coconut milk (p. 17)
1 frozen medium-sized banana
3 tablespoons unsweetened, unsalted almond butter
4 pitted dates
1 tablespoon chia seeds
1 teaspoon maca* powder
½ teaspoon ground cinnamon
a pinch of sea salt

CACAO ALMOND BUTTER CUP

This has been the chocolate smoothie at The Source Cafe since day one. The cacao gives me that boost of energy while it tastes like I'm drinking a chocolate milkshake. Add a scoop of protein powder or a tablespoon of chia seeds for even more nutrition. And if you want this smoothie cold, just freeze your avocado beforehand.

1 ½ cups almond date milk** (p. 16)
2 tablespoons raw cacao powder
2 tablespoons almond butter
¼ avocado, peeled and pitted
4 pitted dates
⅛ teaspoon sea salt
1 drop stevia or 2 tablespoons honey or maple syrup

MATCHA SMOOTHIE

I love any way I can get more matcha into my body, so this smoothie is frequently in my post-workout smoothie rotation. I also love that the coconut oil is good for my metabolism and it helps me stay satiated. I add protein powder to make this a meal substitute.

1 ¼ cups tri nut milk (p. 16)
½ frozen large banana or 1 frozen small banana
a handful of fresh spinach leaves
¼ avocado, peeled and pitted
1 tablespoon coconut oil
1 teaspoon matcha powder
1 teaspoon maca* powder
¼ teaspoon ground cinnamon

Skip the maca if you are pregnant, breastfeeding, or balancing your hormones.
**Substitute ½ cup cold-brewed coffee for ½ cup of the milk if you need more of a buzz.*

GREEN GODDESS BOWL

Makes one 18-ounce bowl

Chlorella is one of my favorite superfoods, and it gives this bowl its rich green color. It's a form of algae that is high in antioxidants, protein, and B vitamins, making it great for energy, brain function, and cell health. But chlorella's real superpower is its function in removing toxins and heavy metals from the body through a process called chelation. The Green Goddess Smoothie Bowl is full of beautiful veggies, but chlorella is the superstar.

¼ cup hemp seed coconut milk (p. 17)
1 cup frozen raw zucchini
½ frozen large banana or 1 frozen small banana
¼ avocado, peeled and pitted
1 handful of fresh spinach leaves
¼ cup vanilla pea protein powder
1 tablespoon tocos powder
½ teaspoon up to 1 tablespoon chlorella powder (start small!)
¼ teaspoon ground cinnamon
Optional: ½ teaspoon dulse

Toppings:
1 tablespoon cacao nibs
1 tablespoon hemp seeds
Or Cinnamon Coconut Pecans (pictured, p. 41)

Combine all of the ingredients in a high-speed blender. Blend until smooth using a tamper, scraping down the sides as you go.

Add more coconut milk as needed to create the consistency you're looking for.

PURPLE SMOOTHIE BOWL

Makes one 18-ounce bowl

Sweet potatoes are my favorite secret weapon in the kitchen. Loaded with nutrients and a sweet, rich flavor, they are the first veggie I started using in my smoothie bowls when I wanted to step away from using fruit all the time.

Anyone can get excited about this purple smoothie bowl simply because it's gorgeous, delicious, and full of protein. The purple sweet potatoes are especially high in antioxidants, and I don't get tired of the amazing color. There's a great boost of healthy fat from the avocado, and you can supercharge this smoothie bowl by adding matcha, chlorella, or your other favorite adaptogens.

½ cup coconut water
1 ¼ cups frozen steamed cauliflower
½ cup frozen roasted purple sweet potato
½ cup frozen blueberries
¼ cup vanilla pea protein powder
¼ avocado, peeled and pitted
2 tablespoons maple syrup or a couple drops of stevia
1 teaspoon maca* powder
1 teaspoon lucuma powder

Toppings:
buckwheat granola (p. 36) or extra berries

Combine all the ingredients in a high-speed blender and blend until smooth, scraping down the sides as you go.

Add more liquid as needed to create the consistency you're looking for.

*Skip the maca if you are pregnant, breastfeeding, or balancing your hormones.

CAULIFLOWER CACAO PEPPERMINT BOWL
WITH TAHINI CRUMBLE

Makes one 18-ounce bowl

If you love a mint-chocolate chip ice cream, you'll love this cacao peppermint bowl. It's been a favorite at the Source Cafe since I added it as a holiday special in the winter of 2018. I only meant to keep it on for the season, but it hasn't left the menu yet. The tahini crumble is lovingly deemed "addictive" by many of our guests. It adds a great texture, resembling cookies and peanut butter cups.

½ cup almond date milk (p. 16)
1 ¼ cups frozen steamed cauliflower
½ cup roasted frozen purple sweet potato
¼ cup vanilla pea protein powder
2 tablespoons raw cacao powder
1 tablespoon tocos powder
1 tablespoon mesquite powder
1 teaspoon maca powder
1 teaspoon lucuma powder
½ teaspoon ground cinnamon
2 drops peppermint essential oil*

Combine all of the ingredients in a high-speed blender and blend until smooth, scraping down the sides as you go. Add more liquid as needed to create the consistency you're looking for. Top with Tahini Crumble, serve and enjoy!

BLACK TAHINI CRUMBLE

Makes 2 cups

It's a common story that the best creations happen by accident. This crumble was the result of a huge mess-up in the kitchen. I was trying to make a protein bar, but got the texture all wrong. The next thing you know, we couldn't stop eating this crumble, and I'm so glad.

1 ¼ cups toasted black tahini**
1 cup dried currants
¼ cup vanilla pea protein powder
2 tablespoons coconut oil
2 tablespoons granulated monk fruit sweetener or 2 tablespoons honey or maple syrup
1 teaspoon ground cinnamon
¼ teaspoon sea salt

Combine the tahini and currants first in a high-speed blender with a tamper. Then add the rest of the ingredients and blend until the mixture is crumbly. If there's any left, store it in an airtight glass container in the fridge.

Always make sure your essential oils are made for internal use.
**The brand I use is Kevala Organic.*

BREAK-FAST

Tip: I often try to maximize my "fasting" time by eating an early dinner and a late-ish breakfast so I can have at least 14 hours when my body isn't doing the work of digestion. Check with your health care team to see if this intermittent fasting could be helpful to you.

breakfast

I'm not sure I agree with the old adage that breakfast is the most important meal of the day. I believe that any time you put food in your body, it's important. However, breakfast is probably my favorite meal, and I believe that the way you start your morning sets the tone for the rest of your day. Most of my mornings begin with a smoothie or a bowl, but there are days that I want a truly hearty breakfast or an indulgent brunch. On those days,

I still prioritize vegetables so I feel healthy and satisfied, knowing I've enjoyed a decadent yet nutritious meal that truly feels good in my body, not just on my taste buds.

Here are some of my all-time favorite breakfast recipes. I'm sharing some unique toasts and cereals as well as my spin on a few classics. I hope they help you start your days out right.

MAPLE TAHINI SWEET POTATO TOAST

Makes 2 servings

This is a sweet, decadent toast that uses a yam or sweet potato instead of bread. This swap is an easy and nutritious grain-free choice. I'm in a long term love affair with tahini, and I replace nut butter with it anywhere I can because I love the earthy flavor of the roasted sesame seeds. But if you're not in love with tahini like I am, you can use any nut butter you like. This recipe calls for a white sweet potato, but you can also use a purple sweet potato, a yam, or whatever bread you have on hand.

Sometimes I like to top this with a small handful of cacao nibs for the extra energy they give me, or ¼ cup of Buckwheat Granola (p. 36) for a nice crunch. However, if I'm going for decadence, I always use the Black Tahini Crumble. (p. 31)

To make a chocolate "Nutella" version of this toast, whisk the maple syrup and tahini together with 2 tablespoons of raw cacao powder. You'll love it!

1 large white sweet potato, peeled
¼ cup roasted tahini
1 banana, peeled and thinly sliced
2 tablespoons maple syrup
½ teaspoon ground cinnamon
Optional: 2 tablespoons cacao powder

Slice the sweet potato lengthwise into pieces about ½-inch thick, or about the thickness of a piece of sandwich bread. You should get at least 4 good-sized slices from one potato.

Toast the slices twice on high in a toaster. If you don't have a toaster, you can roast the slices in a 400-degree oven for 30 minutes, flipping halfway through.

Put the "toast" on a plate and spread the tahini on top. Layer the banana slices on top of the tahini, and finish it with a drizzle of maple syrup and a sprinkle of cinnamon.

Alternative method: For the chocolate version, whisk the tahini, maple syrup, and cacao powder together in a bowl while the potato slices are toasting. Spread the chocolate tahini on the "toast", followed by the bananas and cinnamon, with a little extra maple syrup if you like.

AVOCADO CASHEW TOAST

Makes 1 serving

This toast is hands-down the most popular dish at The Source Cafe. Avocado toast has been en vogue for years now, but this unique version has always impressed avocado toast aficionados.

a thick slice of oat seed bread (p. 47) or whatever bread you have on hand
2 tablespoons cashew cream (p. 108)
¼ avocado, peeled, pitted, and thinly sliced
4 thin slices of radish
a few leaves of parsley
a pinch of sea salt
a teaspoon of flax oil
a pinch of sumac

Toast the slice of oat seed bread to your liking.

Spread the cashew cream over the toast and layer the avocado slices over the cashew cream.

Top with radish slices, parsley leaves, and a sprinkling of salt and sumac. Finish with a drizzle of flax oil.

RED CASHEW & PESTO TOAST

Makes 1 serving

There's a lot of good veggie nutrition on this toast. I like to add some avocado slices or a soft boiled egg on top.

a thick slice of oat seed bread (p. 47) or whatever bread you have on hand
3 tablespoons Red Pepper Cashew Cream (p. 108)
2 tablespoons Arugula Pecan Pesto (p. 107)
A handful of fresh herbs, torn
        (I love using cilantro, mint, basil, parsley, and fennel fronds)
1 teaspoon lemon juice
1 teaspoon olive oil
a pinch of sea salt
Optional: soft boiled egg
Optional: ¼ avocado, peeled, pitted, and sliced

Toast the oat seed bread to your liking and toss the herbs with the lemon, oil, and salt in a small bowl. Spread the Red Pepper Cashew Cream on top of the toast. Add a layer of pesto on top of the cashew cream. (Add your optional avocado or egg.) Then top your toast with the herb mixture.

PISTACHIO & CASHEW CREAM TOAST

Makes 1 serving

Last holiday season, this toast became a favorite at catered events and cooking classes. I like it best with sliced persimmon on top, but persimmon season is short. Enjoy pears, apples, or whatever's in season on top of this toast.

2 slices buckwheat bread (p. 45) or whatever bread you have on hand
1 cup activated cashews
1 cup activated pistachios
¼ cup maple syrup
¼ teaspoon sea salt
a pinch of black pepper
half of a persimmon, sliced
Optional: 1 teaspoon fresh thyme leaves
Optional: 2 tablespoons Cinnamon Coconut Pecans (p. 41)

Blend the nuts, maple syrup, salt, pepper, and thyme in a food processor until creamy, about 90 seconds.

Toast the slice of buckwheat bread either in a toaster and spread a big spoonful of the creamy nut butter on the toast and top with a few slices of persimmon.

Finish with the Cinnamon Coconut Pecans for a little crunch.

BUCKWHEAT GRANOLA

Makes 3 cups

breakfast

I originally created this granola as part of a breakfast parfait, but for years now I've been eating it like trail mix, topping smoothie bowls with it, and enjoying it as a snack. It's sugarless unless you add some maple syrup, and it has great flavor and a perfect crunch. The nuts, seeds, and buckwheat groats provide high fiber, plant protein, omega-3 fatty acids, and healthy fats. I never feel guilty about enjoying a large handful of this beautiful granola. Try the chocolate version as well for a healthy treat.

1 cup buckwheat groats
½ cup activated pecans
½ cup activated pumpkin seeds
½ cup activated sliced almonds
3 tablespoons unsweetened shredded coconut
2 tablespoons coconut oil
1 teaspoon ground cinnamon
¼ teaspoon salt
Optional: 3 tablespoons maple syrup
Optional: ¼ cups vegan chocolate chips

Preheat the oven to 350 degrees and line a sheet pan with parchment paper. Mix all the ingredients together in a bowl. (If you're making chocolate granola, don't add the chocolate chips yet.) Spread the mixture onto the parchment-lined sheet pan, and bake in the oven for 15-18 minutes until golden, carefully stirring halfway through.

Remove the pan from the oven. (If you're making the chocolate version, pour the granola into a bowl right away and stir in the chocolate chips.) When cool, enjoy, and store leftovers in glass jars at room temperature for up to two weeks.

OVERNIGHT BANANA OATMEAL

Makes 4 servings

This oatmeal has been a favorite Source Cafe to-go item for several years. I'm proud that this oatmeal has stood the test of time. It's not just the convenience that makes it a favorite. The flavor, texture, and health benefits keep people coming back for it day after day.

I love the ease of overnight oats. The preparation is really quick, so with a little forethought, you can have a delicious and nutritious breakfast even on a rushed morning.

Substitutions: Feel free to substitute any nut or seed butter for the almond butter. You can also substitute honey for the maple syrup. Change out the bananas for a seasonal fruit if you want. Isn't life easier when you can just use what you have in the house? I try to make these recipes easy to play with, so have fun with it.

2 ½ cups gluten-free oats
2 cups coconut water
1 banana, peeled
5 tablespoons maple syrup
¼ cup almond butter
2 tablespoons flax meal
2 tablespoons chia seeds
2 teaspoons vanilla extract
1 teaspoon ground cinnamon

The night before, combine all of the ingredients in a food processor and blend together until creamy. Let the oatmeal sit overnight in the fridge for the full soaking benefits. The mixture will look a little liquidy, but don't worry, it will thicken as it sits overnight.

The next morning, serve bowls of oatmeal topped with seeds, nuts, buckwheat granola, or your favorite fruit.

PALEO PORRIDGE

Makes 6 servings

Porridge can be full of sugar, but this fast and easy porridge is loaded with healthy fats, fiber, and protein instead. If I want even more protein to sustain me through a busy day, I'll add a scoop of collagen powder or protein powder. I make a full batch of this porridge and keep it in the fridge for the week, heating up a portion at a time. (I've been known to eat it cold right from the fridge, too.)

If you're not sure how much of this you'll eat in a week, you can make it last longer by combining all the ingredients except the water and maple syrup in a large airtight glass jar. The dry mixture will store for up to three months. When you're ready for breakfast, just blend ½ cup of the dry mixture with ¾ cup of boiling water. Sweeten with maple syrup to taste, and add up to another ¼ cup of boiling water to make your porridge thinner.

3 cups boiling water, more for a thinner porridge
3 tablespoons maple syrup
1 tablespoon plus 1 ½ teaspoons coconut oil, melted
¾ cup activated pecans
¾ cup activated walnuts
½ cup activated almonds
¼ cup activated brazil nuts
¼ cup shredded unsweetened shredded coconut
2 pitted dates
2 tablespoons flax meal
1 tablespoon lucuma powder
2 teaspoons ground cinnamon
1/4 teaspoon sea salt
Optional: Cinnamon Coconut Pecans (p. 41), extra coconut, or fresh berries

Combine all the ingredients in a high-speed blender and blend until smooth, 60-90 seconds, scraping down the sides as you go.

If you want a thinner oatmeal, add more boiling water, a tablespoon at a time.
Top each serving with extra coconut, Cinnamon Coconut Pecans, or fresh berries.

Store leftovers in the fridge for up to a week.

WHY SOAK OATS OVERNIGHT?

Soaking oats overnight breaks down the starches and reduces phytic acid, making the oats easier to digest. Our bodies can also absorb more nutrients from soaked oats. I always want the most nutrition possible from my food, and I never want to compromise optimal digestion. Since it's so beneficial and easy to do, I always soak my oats now, and never feel the bloating I use to feel from oatmeal.

CAULIFLOWER "OATMEAL"
WITH ROASTED BANANAS

Makes 4 servings

For the oatmeal:
1 large head of cauliflower or 4 cups riced cauliflower
1 ½ cups hemp seed coconut milk (p. 17)
½ cup filtered water
2 medium-sized bananas
¼ cup vanilla pea protein powder
2 tablespoons vanilla extract
1 tablespoon psyllium husk powder
1 tablespoon ground cinnamon
¼ teaspoon sea salt
Optional: ¼ cup maple syrup or 3 drops of stevia

For the topping:
2 large bananas
1 tablespoon coconut oil, melted
½ teaspoon ground turmeric
½ teaspoon ground cinnamon
A handful of unsweetened shredded coconut, for serving

All the recipes in this book are designed to help you incorporate more vegetables into your diet. In the kitchen, I'm often daydreaming about how to turn the vegetables I already love into delicious, surprising, sexy dishes you'll crave. This "oatmeal" was born of one of those kitchen daydream sessions.

The cauliflower is a quite satisfying and hearty substitute for oats, and the vanilla, cinnamon, and banana bring the flavor that makes this breakfast anything but boring. Psyllium husk adds fiber, and protein powder makes it a substantial meal. I make mine without any sugar, but you can add maple syrup or stevia if you prefer some sweetness. It's also delicious served cold like rice pudding. Put any leftovers into small single-serving jars, and refrigerate for up to four days.

Preheat the oven to 400 degrees and line a sheet pan with parchment paper. While the oven is preheating, peel the bananas for the topping and slice them into 1-inch thick pieces. Whisk the cinnamon, turmeric and melted coconut oil together in a large bowl, then toss the banana pieces in the spiced oil until coated. Place the banana pieces on the prepared sheet pan and roast for 20 minutes.

If you're starting with a head of cauliflower, cut it into small florets and pulse them in small batches in a food processor until the cauliflower is finely chopped, resembling grains of rice.

Combine 4 cups of riced cauliflower with coconut milk in a medium-sized pot with a lid, and bring it to a boil over high heat. Once boiling, reduce the heat to medium-low.

Cook on medium-low, covered, for 8 minutes and then remove from heat.

Scoop one cup of the cauliflower mixture into a high-speed blender. Add the 2 bananas, protein powder, psyllium husk, salt, vanilla, cinnamon, and water, and blend until smooth.

Pour the blended mixture back into the pot with the rest of the cooked cauliflower. Cook for another 10 minutes on medium-low heat, constantly stirring.

Serve the oatmeal warm, topped with the roasted bananas, shredded coconut, and a sprinkle of cinnamon.

FRITTATA

Makes 6 servings

8 eggs
1 cup coconut milk
1 cup seasonal squash
¼ cup pumpkin seeds
1 small leek, sliced
1 cup Swiss chard, roughly chopped
2 cloves of garlic, diced
6 basil leaves, finely chopped
1 teaspoon sumac
¾ teaspoon sea salt
½ teaspoon ground black pepper
½ cup cashew cream (p. 108)

There's nothing like the comfort of a well made frittata. This crowd-pleaser is full of flavor, so it's great for something like a Sunday brunch. Your guests will definitely be asking for seconds. One of my favorite things about a frittata is that you can enjoy it hot, cold, or at room temperature... and you can use any leftover veggies you have around. There's no bad way to eat a frittata. This recipe calls for seasonal squash (delicata and kabocha are my favorites!), but if there's none available, butternut squash will do. Just cut it into ½-inch thick pieces. You can also substitute any available veggies like broccoli or asparagus. Frittatas are adaptable!

Preheat the oven to 350 degrees. Coat a 9-inch cast-iron skillet or an 8x8-inch casserole pan with coconut oil or avocado oil.

Add the oil, garlic, squash or veggies, leek, Swiss chard, salt, and pepper to a sauté pan or your cast iron skillet, and cook over medium heat for 5 minutes until just softened. Remove from heat, and transfer the ingredients to a medium-sized bowl.

In a separate large bowl, whisk the eggs, coconut milk and sumac together, then whisk in the pumpkin seeds and basil. Add the warm veggies to the bowl and mix well. Pour the whole mixture into the prepared pan and top it with tablespoon-sized dollops of cashew cream spaced evenly.

Bake for 25 to 30 minutes until the egg is set and doesn't jiggle in the middle. Top with more chopped basil before serving.

PROTEIN PANCAKES
WITH CINNAMON COCONUT PECANS

Makes 10-12 pancakes

Dry Ingredients:
2 ½ cups gluten-free flour
3 tablespoons flax meal
2 tablespoons baking powder
2 teaspoons ground cinnamon
¼ cup vanilla pea protein powder
½ teaspoon sea salt

Wet Ingredients:
2 bananas
3 tablespoons coconut oil
1 teaspoon vanilla extract
1 ½ cups hemp seed coconut milk
or whatever milk you have on
hand
1 cup water

Breakfast for dinner was a special-occasion treat when I was growing up, so it always feels like a celebration when I enjoy pancakes. But as I get older and wiser, it's less enjoyable to eat boxed-mix pancakes loaded with butter and fake syrup. I was eager to find a way to eat pancakes without the sugar crash and actually fuel my body with nutrition at the same time.

These pancakes are also great as an on-the-go snack, so you can always make them and refrigerate them for the next day. The batter also stores well for up to a week, so you can make a batch of batter, keep it in the fridge, and fry them up one or two at a time throughout the week.

Sharing these with my family and yours really warms my heart. I hope you enjoy them as much as I do.

About the Toppings: I top these pancakes with Almond Butter Syrup and Cinnamon Coconut Pecans. The Cinnamon Coconut Pecans are also great as a gift, or on top of oatmeal. The almond butter syrup lasts four weeks in the fridge and is delicious on top of a smoothie bowl.

To make the pancakes, whisk together all the dry ingredients in a large bowl and set it aside. Combine the bananas, coconut oil, vanilla, and coconut milk in a high-speed blender, and blend until smooth.

Whisk the wet ingredients into the dry ingredients until they're well-combined, but careful not to over-mix.

Spray or coat a small pan with 1 teaspoon coconut oil or avocado oil and put over medium heat. When the pan is hot enough that a drop of water dances in the pan, scoop ¼ cup of pancake batter into the pan and cook for 2 minutes. Then turn over with a spatula and cook for another 2 minutes on the other side. Remove from the pan and top with almond butter syrup and pecans.

ALMOND BUTTER SYRUP

½ cup water at room temperature
½ cup creamy almond butter at room temperature
¼ cup maple syrup at room temperature or ¼ cup granulated monk fruit sweetener
½ teaspoon ground cinnamon

To make the syrup, whisk together the water, almond butter, maple syrup or monk fruit, and cinnamon in a small mixing bowl until they've combined to make a smooth syrup that will drizzle easily.

CINNAMON COCONUT PECANS

1 cup activated raw pecans
1 cup unsweetened shredded coconut
¼ cup coconut oil, melted
3 tablespoons maple syrup
2 teaspoons ground cinnamon
a pinch of sea salt

To make the pecans, preheat the oven to 350 degrees and line a sheet pan with parchment paper. Whisk the coconut oil, maple syrup, cinnamon, and shredded coconut together in a small mixing bowl. Toss in the pecans and stir until they're coated. Pour the coated pecans onto the parchment-lined sheet pan, spreading them so they're not in large clumps. Bake for 25 minutes then remove from the oven.

SMOKED SALMON BENEDICT
WITH COCONUT HOLLANDAISE SAUCE

Makes 4 servings

6 cups filtered water
2 tablespoons white vinegar
8 eggs
8 slices oat seed bread (p. 47)
4 tablespoons plant-based butter
8 ounces wild smoked salmon
1 head of frisée
fresh cracked black pepper
Optional: Fermented Veggies (p. 107)

When you want an indulgent brunch, try this Smoked Salmon Benedict. It delivers all the richness of Eggs Benedict with a few healthier twists. The poached egg stays the same, but I use wild salmon, nutritious bread, and dairy-free hollandaise to enjoy this classic without an ounce of guilt.

You can use any bread you like, but I love making this with the gluten-free seed bread. If it's already made, I'll just toast up a few slices. But if I'm making the bread just for this recipe, I'll form it into 4- or 5-inch patties before baking, so they're shaped like English Muffins.

The bright, lemony hollandaise sauce perfectly cuts through the richness of the smoked salmon, and it's just a quick variation on the Coconut Aioli. I always recommend using wild salmon so you avoid the dyes used in farmed fish.

COCONUT HOLLANDAISE SAUCE

½ cup Coconut Aioli (p. 105) or Classic Egg Aioli (p. 105)
1 garlic clove, chopped
2 tablespoons lemon juice
¼ teaspoon ground turmeric
¼ teaspoon sea salt
3 tablespoons water, plus more as needed

First, combine the coconut aioli, garlic, lemon juice, turmeric, and salt in a blender. Blend, adding a tablespoon of water at a time until the sauce is runny like a traditional hollandaise. Set the sauce aside until it's time to serve. (Note: The sauce will thicken and harden once refrigerated. To refresh it, let it sit at room temperature for 30 minutes, then whisk to create a smooth texture. Alternatively, you can blend it again in the blender.)

For the poached eggs: Heat 6 cups of water in a shallow pot. Once boiling, reduce heat to low and add the vinegar. Crack an egg into a small bowl and gently pour it into the water, getting as close to the surface of the water as possible before adding the egg. Repeat with the remaining eggs. Cook for 3-4 minutes or until the whites have set and the yolk is still soft. Remove with a slotted spoon onto a paper-towel-lined plate to dry off slightly.

Meanwhile, toast the bread and then spread the ghee or butter on top.

Pile 1 or 2 pieces of smoked salmon on each piece of toast, and a poached egg on top of the salmon.

Drizzle the hollandaise over the egg, and add a small pile of the frisee leaves on top. Finish with a bit of cracked black pepper, and an optional tablespoon of fermented veggies.

I'm not one for tricky recipes that you have to get "just right." I do not have the precision of a baker; I am a chef through and through. Some breads require skill and exactitude, but none of the breads in this chapter are like that. I love making nutritious breads that are easy and quick to make. I mix the dough for most of these right in my food processor. There's no yeast, no rising, and no way you can mess it up. Give these different breads a try, and as always: get creative to make them suit your taste.

Note: In these recipes, when wet and dry ingredients are mixed separately, or if there are distinct steps with different groups of ingredients, I've separated and ordered the ingredients list to make it as easy as possible to follow.

breads

BUCKWHEAT BREAD
WITH BERRY CHIA SEED COMPOTE

Makes 1 loaf

Dry Ingredients:
1 ½ cups almond flour
1 cup buckwheat flour
3 tablespoons psyllium husk powder
2 tablespoons chia seeds
2 tablespoons hemp seeds
2 teaspoons baking soda
¼ teaspoon sea salt
¼ cup fresh rosemary, chopped
¾ cups dried currants (or any other dried berry)

Wet Ingredients:
2 cups water
3 tablespoons apple cider vinegar
2 tablespoons maple syrup

BERRY CHIA SEED COMPOTE

3 cups strawberries, de-stemmed and roughly chopped
1 cup raspberries
Juice from 1 orange (about 3 tablespoons)
2 tablespoons maple syrup
1 teaspoon vanilla extract
1 tablespoon chia seeds

People are always surprised by how healthy this bread is. It's a great source of plant protein, and is very high in fiber, omega-3 fatty acids, and healthy fats. Beloved by all, you'd be hard pressed to find someone who can't eat it. It's gluten-free, dairy-free, plant-based, egg-free, and yeast-free. The best part about this bread is that you can add in different herbs, fruits, and nuts to give it a new personality. This recipe is for a rosemary-currant version, but you can alter those ingredients for a whole new bread. Try a savory bread by using 1 tablespoon chopped garlic, ¼ cup chopped olives, and 2 tablespoons thyme, or ½ cup chopped sundried tomatoes, ¼ cup chopped walnuts, and ¼ cup rosemary.

Preheat the oven to 350 degrees. In a mixing bowl, whisk together the dry ingredients except for the rosemary and currants, and break up any lumps. Then add the rosemary and currants, whisking to incorporate.

In a separate bowl, whisk the maple syrup, apple cider vinegar, and water together.

Pour the wet ingredients slowly into the dry ingredients and mix thoroughly with a wooden spoon until a dough forms. Cover the dough with a damp towel and let it sit for an hour so the psyllium husk and chia seeds can thicken the dough.

Coat a loaf pan with coconut oil. Put the dough into the pan and tap the pan hard on the counter a few times to make sure all the air bubbles come to the top, so the bread will bake evenly throughout.

Bake the bread for 80 minutes and let it cool a full 30 minutes before removing it from the pan.

To make the compote:
While the bread is baking, set aside the chia seeds and put the rest of the compote ingredients into a medium-sized soup pot. Cook, covered, over low heat for 30 minutes, stirring occasionally. Then turn the heat off and stir in the chia seeds. Let sit for about 15 minutes until the compote takes on a gel-like texture.

Once the bread is cool, slice a piece about 1-inch thick and spread the compote on top. Enjoy for breakfast or as a hearty snack.

Store leftover bread and compote in airtight containers in the fridge for up to a week. You can also freeze slices of bread and defrost them later. These slices defrost best by sitting out at room temperature.

PALEO PROTEIN SNACK BREAD

Makes 1 loaf

This is the ultimate quick-to-make, impossible-to-mess-up, full-of-protein bread. It takes less than ten minutes to prepare, and less than 20 minutes to bake. Including cooling time, you could be eating this bread 45 minutes after you started it.

In addition to how fast it is to prepare, I love the protein and fiber in this bread. I much prefer a piece of this homemade bread to a sugary protein bar from the store when I'm hungry and in a rush. Like the Buckwheat Bread, the flavor of this bread is versatile. Try adding a handful of herbs, orange zest, chopped olives, and nuts. Or for a sweeter bread, substitute a vanilla protein powder and add ½ cup of dried blueberries. Get creative and have fun – the options are endless!

This bread is great on its own, but it's also perfect for little tapas or sandwiches. I love to top it with pistachio pesto (p. 106) and a slice of avocado, or with the almond butter syrup (p. 41) and sliced fruit. I've also used individual slices to make a hearty French toast.

Wet Ingredients:
1 ½ cups almond flour
½ cup unflavored pea protein
powder or another ½ cup almond
flour
¼ cup flax meal
2 tablespoons coconut flour
¼ teaspoon sea salt
¼ teaspoon baking soda
5 eggs

Dry Ingredients:
1 tablespoon coconut oil plus
more for coating the pan
2 tablespoons olive oil
1 tablespoon apple cider vinegar
1 tablespoon honey
Zest from 1 lemon

Preheat the oven to 350 degrees. Coat a loaf pan with coconut oil.

In a food processor, combine all of the wet ingredients and pulse for 30 seconds. Add all of the dry ingredients and blend for a minute until the dough is smooth. Place the dough in the loaf pan and bake for 15-18 minutes until golden brown. It's ready when a toothpick inserted into the middle comes out clean. Let cool for 15 minutes before slicing.

OAT SEED BREAD

Makes 2 loaves

1 cup buckwheat groats
3 cups hot water

½ cup psyllium husk powder
3 more cups filtered water

2 ½ cups gluten-free oats, divided
²/₃ cup millet flour
¼ cup coconut oil, melted
2 tablespoons baking powder
2 ¼ teaspoons sea salt

3 tablespoons assorted seeds (I use chia, flax, and hemp)
1 tablespoon melted coconut oil to coat the pan

You have to think ahead for this bread, because the buckwheat groats need to soak in water overnight. But this delicious bread is gluten-free, plant-based, egg-free, yeast-free, and nut-free. I take special pride when I create something that almost everyone can enjoy. Top this bread with nut butter, avocado, or egg salad, and you have a complete, balanced meal. I love the crunchy crust and the extra fiber that comes from the psyllium husk. Bonus: this bread holds moisture for days, so don't be afraid to store it (in the fridge) for a week.

Place the buckwheat groats in a large bowl and stir in 3 cups of hot water. Cover and refrigerate overnight. The next day, drain the soaked groats and rinse very well until the water runs clear.

Preheat the oven to 350 degrees. Coat two loaf pans with coconut oil. Place the psyllium husk in a large bowl and cover with 3 cups of water. Whisk thoroughly, then set aside for 15 minutes.

Meanwhile, combine the rinsed buckwheat groats, melted coconut oil, millet flour, 1 ½ cups oats, baking powder, and salt in a food processor until smooth, at least 30 seconds.

Add the soaked psyllium husk to the food processor and process together until the mixture is well combined.

Add the remaining 1 cup of oats and pulse the mixture 10 times or until mixed well, scraping the sides as you go. The dough will be very thick.

Transfer half of the dough into one of the prepared pans, and the other half of the dough into the other pan. Using wet hands, press the dough evenly into the pans. The dough should be thick and sticky.

Sprinkle the assorted seeds over the top of the loaf and press down with your hands to set the seeds.

Place both loaf pans in the oven and bake for 40 minutes to start.

Carefully remove the bread and use a small, sharp knife to score the bread, cutting ¼- inch deep lines diagonally across the bread and then the other direction to create a diamond-shaped pattern to remove any air bubbles that are forming in the dough.

Return the bread to the oven and bake for another 30-40 minutes until it's firm to the touch. A tester inserted into the center of the bread should come out clean. Let cool for 30 minutes in the pan before turning out onto a wire rack. Let cool completely before slicing.

BEET BLUEBERRY MUFFIN

Makes 18 muffins

1 large beet or 1¾ cups beet puree
¼ cup full-fat coconut milk
¼ cup filtered water
3 tablespoons lemon juice
2 teaspoons apple cider vinegar
2 cups gluten-free flour
2 teaspoons baking soda
2 teaspoons baking powder
1 teaspoon xanthan gum
1 teaspoon sea salt
½ cup plus 2 tablespoons granulated monk fruit sweetener*
½ cup olive oil
1 teaspoon vanilla extract
1 cup fresh or frozen blueberries
melted coconut oil for coating the muffin pan

Why make a plain blueberry muffin when you can sneak in some sexy beets for added nutrition and beauty? I'm always looking for tasty, satisfying, and unexpected ways to boost the nutrition of a dish. Roasted beets not only give these beautiful muffins their unique color, but they also bring fiber and magnesium to the table while helping to lower blood pressure and decrease inflammation. Not bad for a breakfast treat, right? This is a recipe I developed for the opening of The Source Cafe. We made dozens of batches before we perfected the taste and texture. I love my job!

Preheat the oven to 375 degrees. If you're starting with a whole beet, cut the stalk off and cut it in half. Wrap it tightly in a foil "packet" and roast for 45 minutes until very tender. Remove it from the oven, open the foil packet, and let it cool. Reduce the oven temperature to 350 degrees.

When the beet is cool enough to touch, use a paper towel to rub the skin off each half. Puree the roasted beet in a food processor until very smooth, about 2-3 minutes. (You'll use 1 ¾ cups of the beet puree for this recipe. Any remaining puree can be used for soups or smoothies.)

Coat the wells of a muffin pan with melted coconut oil.

Whisk together the coconut milk, lemon juice, and apple cider vinegar in a small bowl. Set aside for at least 10 minutes so the vinegar, lemon juice and milk curdle to create a buttermilk substitute.

In a large bowl, combine the flour, baking soda, baking powder, xanthan gum, and sea salt, whisking to combine. Pour the wet mixture into the dry mixture and whisk until very smooth.

Stir in the pureed beets, mixing thoroughly, and then fold in the blueberries.

Scoop ¼ cup of batter into each muffin well, making 18 even-sized muffins. (If you're making jumbo-sized muffins, use ½ cup of the batter.)

Bake for 18-22 minutes, until a toothpick inserted into the center of the muffins comes out clean.

Remove from the oven and let cool at least 30 minutes before serving.

*If you don't like granulated monk fruit sweetener, you can substitute ¾ cup plus 1 tablespoon coconut sugar.

BANANA CHOCOLATE CHIP MUFFINS

Makes 12 muffins

This version of the classic muffin has been the favorite at The Source Cafe, selling out since day one. For this book, I changed this recipe to use granulated monk fruit sweetener instead of sugar, and I think it works really well. But if you prefer sugar, the substitution is listed below. This batter saves very well in the fridge, so you can bake the whole batch at once, or bake them a few at a time if you can't be trusted with 12 muffins in the house. The batter will last 4 days.

Dry Ingredients:
2 cups gluten-free flour
2 teaspoons baking soda
2 teaspoons baking powder
1 teaspoon xanthan gum
1 teaspoon sea salt

Wet Ingredients:
1 cup plus 2 tablespoons water
½ cup coconut oil, melted
¼ cup granulated monk fruit sweetener*
1 ½ teaspoon vanilla extract
1 ¼ cups mashed bananas
½ cup chocolate chips

Preheat the oven to 350 degrees.

Coat the wells of a 12-muffin pan with coconut oil.

In a large mixing bowl, whisk all the dry ingredients together. In a separate medium-sized mixing bowl, whisk all of the wet ingredients together. Add the wet ingredients into the dry ingredients, and whisk together until creamy.

Fold in the mashed bananas and the chocolate chips. Scoop ¼ cup into each of 12 muffin wells.

Bake for 18 minutes or firm to the touch.

*If you don't like granulated monk fruit sweetener, you can substitute ½ cup organic cane sugar.

PUMPKIN BREAD

Makes 1 large loaf

2 ¹/₃ cups gluten-free flour
1 ¼ cups granulated monk fruit sweetener*
1 ½ teaspoons baking soda
1 teaspoon xanthan gum
1 teaspoon sea salt
¾ teaspoon ground cloves
¾ teaspoon ground cinnamon
½ teaspoon ground nutmeg
½ teaspoon baking powder
1 ¹/₃ cups pure pumpkin puree**
3 large eggs
¼ cup plus 2 tablespoons water
²/₃ cups olive oil

When this bread is in the oven and the house smells like pumpkin and spices, I immediately think of my Grandma. I remember waking up early in the morning to this smell as a child and running into the kitchen to beat my sister and cousins to get the first bite. I cannot begin to tell you how much of this bread I have eaten over the years! When I opened The Source, I knew it had to be part of the menu, and it's been the most requested item ever since. I may have turned this into an unrefined sugar and gluten-free bread, but this will always be my Grandma's bread. We spent hours making pumpkin bread and cherry pies with the fresh cherries from her tree. Every time I take a bite of this bread I am reminded that I would not be the chef I am today without her early inspiration. Thanks, Grandma!

Preheat the oven to 350 degrees.

Coat a loaf pan with melted coconut oil, making sure you get the oil into each of the corners. In a large bowl, whisk together the flour, sugar, baking soda, xanthan gum, salt, cloves, cinnamon, nutmeg, and baking powder.

In another large bowl, whisk together the pumpkin puree, eggs, water, and olive oil.

Add the dry mixture to the wet mixture, whisking by hand until there are no lumps.

Pour the batter into the prepared pan and bake for 35 minutes. Rotate the pan and bake for another 20-25 minutes until a toothpick inserted into the thickest part comes out clean.

Let the bread cool inside the pan on a rack for 30 minutes. Then carefully turn it out of the pan onto a wire rack and let cool completely before slicing.

*If you don't like granulated monk fruit sweetener, you can substitute 1 ¾ cups organic cane sugar
**When there was a shortage of organic pumpkin puree, we made a sweet potato puree that substituted beautifully.

I just love a warm bowl of soup on a gray day. Although we usually have beautiful sunny days where I live, we often have gray mornings, so I'm usually in the mood for soup by lunchtime. Sometimes my soup is just veggies and a blender, but I've given you a variety of recipes here to get a taste of my favorites. As always, feel free to substitute what you have on hand. Nothing makes a better soup than leftover veggies.

soups

MY FAVORITE GREEN SOUP

Makes 4-6 servings

1 ½ cups broccoli, roughly chopped
1 ½ small zucchinis, roughly chopped
½ bunch of kale, de-stemmed and roughly chopped
½ medium-sized yellow onion, roughly chopped
2 large carrots, peeled and roughly chopped
4 garlic cloves, peeled
1 tablespoon fresh ginger root, skin on, chopped
1 tablespoon fresh turmeric root, skin on, chopped
1 teaspoons sea salt
½ teaspoon ground black pepper
½ teaspoon ground cinnamon
juice from ½ lemon (about 1 tablespoon)
3 cups water
olive oil for topping

Warning: this delicious soup is not the prettiest color. It's a deep, dark brownish-green, but it's so yummy and nutritious, I don't care how it looks! It's a truly versatile soup that tastes great on its own or with some ground bison for added protein. If I'm staying away from oil, I'll even use this soup to sauté vegetables or poach fish. If you want a creamier soup, just add a splash of coconut milk. This green soup has been a staple meal for me for years, and keeps my body alkalized and balanced. Now my family and friends regularly keep some green soup in the freezer, too, defrosting it when they crave it. Double this recipe and blend in batches if you want to have leftovers to freeze, or if you're cooking for a large family.

Because this is a blended soup, all of the veggies can be roughly chopped into large pieces. My secret ingredient is the cinnamon, which together with the ginger and turmeric gives it a little kick and a more complex flavor.

My favorite toppings for this soup are chopped avocado and pumpkin seeds, a spoonful of chlorella, some coconut milk, or extra veggies.

Put all of the ingredients in a medium-sized soup pot and bring to a boil over high heat. Then reduce the heat to medium, cover, and cook for 45 minutes.

Remove the pot from the heat and transfer the soup into a high-speed blender. Blend until the soup is smooth and creamy. Add salt and pepper to taste.

Serve each bowl with a drizzle of olive oil, and any toppings you like.

KABOCHA SQUASH
COCONUT CREAM SOUP

Makes 4-6 servings

2 small kabocha squashes, or 3 cups chopped frozen squash
1 fennel bulb, chopped
1 small sweet yellow onion, chopped
3 cups water
1 cup coconut milk
2 ½ teaspoons sea salt, divided
¼ teaspoon ground cardamom
¼ teaspoon ground black pepper
5 tablespoons melted coconut oil, divided
½ cup pumpkin seeds for topping

When squash season comes, I can't wait to get my hands on kabocha squash and make this soup. I love it so much that I even use leftover soup as a sauce on fish or bison. I can't get enough of it!

Preheat the oven to 400 degrees and line three sheet pans with parchment paper. One of them can be a half sheet pan, or the sheet pan from a toaster oven.

Cut the kabocha squash into halves, then into eight wedges, and scrape out the seeds with a spoon and discard them.

Toss the squash wedges, skin on, with 2 tablespoons of coconut oil and ½ teaspoon salt.

Place the squash wedges on a full-size sheet pan and roast for 35 minutes until fork-tender.

While the squash is roasting, toss the chopped fennel and onion likewise with 2 tablespoons of coconut oil and ½ teaspoon of salt. Spread the fennel and onion on the other full-size sheet pan and roast for 20 minutes until just brown.

Toss the pumpkin seeds with a tablespoon of coconut oil and a pinch of salt, and spread them on the third smaller sheet pan. Toast in the oven for 10 minutes.
When the squash is done and cool enough to touch, use a knife to remove the squash from its skin.

Blend the roasted squash, onion, and fennel with the remaining ingredients in a high-speed blender until the soup is smooth and creamy. Slowly add more water, a tablespoon at a time, for a thinner soup.

Top each bowl of soup with the toasted seeds and a drizzle of olive oil.

*I use full-fat coconut milk from a can.

YAM FENNEL SOUP

Makes 4-6 servings

This blended yam soup has been a staple at The Source since opening day. To make life easier, I make large batches of soup and freeze single portions so I have them when I need them. This soup is great on its own or topped with some pecans and slices of avocado. Pair this with a slice of toasted oat seed bread covered in pesto for a perfect warm meal. All the ingredients can be chopped roughly for this recipe because they all end up in the blender. I love how quick and easy this soup is. I hope you love its simple beauty, too.

1 ½ medium-sized yams, peeled and chopped roughly into about 1-inch pieces
½ fennel bulb, chopped
¼ small yellow onion, diced
2 tablespoons cashew cream (p. 108)
juice from ½ lemon (about 1 tablespoon)
1 ½ teaspoons sea salt
¾ teaspoons ground turmeric
1/8 teaspoon ground black pepper
4 ½ cups water
1 cup pecans for topping
¼ cup olive oil, divided

Preheat the oven to 350 degrees and line three sheet pans with parchment paper. One of them can be a half sheet pan, or the sheet pan from a toaster oven. Toss the chopped yams in a bowl with 2 tablespoons of olive oil and a pinch of salt. Spread the coated yams on one of the prepared sheet pans, and roast for 20 minutes until they're just golden brown.

As soon as the yams are in the oven, toss the onion and fennel the same way with 2 tablespoons of olive oil and a pinch of salt. Spread them on the other sheet pan and roast for 15 minutes.

Spread the pecans on the third smaller sheet pan and toast them in the oven for 15 minutes.

Once the veggies are done, add all of the ingredients to a high-speed blender and blend for about a minute, until the soup is smooth and creamy.

Serve each bowl topped with some toasted pecans and a drizzle of olive oil.

CAULIFLOWER COCONUT SOUP

Makes 4-6 servings

This soup reminds me of the decadent, creamy potato soup I used to enjoy as a kid. But those heavy, cream-based, cheesy soups really upset my stomach now. There's no need to add cream or cheese to this soup because the cauliflower and white sweet potato give it a creamy texture.

The sweet potato gives this soup a sweeter flavor. If you prefer a more traditional tasting soup, use regular white potato instead. For a cheesier tasting soup, stir ¼ cup of nutritional yeast into the finished soup. I like to dress each bowl up with a dollop of cashew cream, some pumpkin seeds, and a few slices of avocado.

1 large white sweet potato, peeled and cubed
1 ½ heads of cauliflower, chopped, or 6 cups cauliflower florets
1 small yellow onion
3 cloves garlic
4 cups coconut milk
1 cup water
2 teaspoons sea salt
1 teaspoon ground black pepper
juice from 1 orange (about 3 tablespoons)
juice from 1 lemon (about 2 tablespoons)
sumac for topping
Optional for topping: cashew cream, seeds, avocado, nutritional yeast

Put all the ingredients except the lemon and orange juices in a soup pot, and bring to a boil over high heat. Once boiling, lower the heat and cover, cooking for 35 minutes until the veggies are tender.

Then remove from the heat and transfer half the contents of the pot to a high-speed blender, blending the first batch until smooth and creamy. Transfer the first batch to a bowl and blend the other half. Then combine both batches.

Finally, whisk in the lemon and orange juices.

Top each bowl with sumac and your choice of nuts or seeds.

CHESTNUT CREAM SOUP

Makes 4-6 servings

2 tablespoons plant-based butter
2 shallots, roughly chopped
2 cloves garlic, roughly chopped
2 stalks celery, roughly chopped
½ pound mushrooms, quartered
1 14-ounce jar of vacuum roasted chestnuts, roughly chopped (Save 6 chestnuts for garnish)
4 cups vegetable broth or bone broth
¼ cup white wine
2 bay leaves
1 sprig of thyme
2 teaspoons sea salt
½ teaspoon ground black pepper
2 ½ cups coconut milk
1 cup water

I get so excited when it's chestnut season because this soup really does warm my heart and soul. An earlier version of this soup was a coveted New Year's Eve tradition at one of my first restaurants, but in those days I made it with heavy whipping cream. I love this version with coconut milk and plant-based butter made from cashews. It's the perfect start to any holiday season meal, and it pairs beautifully with a glass of champagne or rosé.

Put the vegan butter, garlic, and shallots in a medium-sized soup pot over medium heat and sauté for 2 minutes.

Add the celery, mushrooms, and chestnuts and cook for 5 minutes more.

Then add the white wine and cook for about 5 minutes, until the wine has almost evaporated.

Add the broth, herbs, salt, pepper, and ½ cup of coconut milk.

Continue cooking over medium heat for 30 minutes.
Remove the pot from the heat and use a slotted spoon to remove the bay leaves and sprig of thyme.

Add half the contents of the pot plus half the water and 1 cup of the coconut milk to a blender, and blend until the soup is creamy. Transfer from the blender to a new pot, and blend the remaining contents of the pot, the water, and coconut milk into the blender, blending until creamy. Combine the two batches in the pot and stir together. Serve topped with chopped chestnuts, a few fresh thyme leaves, and a pinch of sumac.

*I use full-fat coconut milk from a can.

HEALING BROTH

Makes 4-6 servings

I started drinking this broth when I was working with a functional doctor to heal my adrenals. When I drink this broth, I swear I can feel it healing me. I love that in addition to helping with adrenal function, the cilantro helps to pull toxic heavy metals from my body. I drink this broth by itself, (hot or cold) but I also use it as a liquid when I make rice or as the base for a savory smoothie or a warm herbal tea.

1 white sweet potato, peeled and chopped
2 stalks celery, chopped
1 yellow onion, chopped
4 cloves garlic whole, peeled
1 bunch dandelion greens, roughly chopped
1 fennel bulb, chopped
1 bunch of parsley, stems on, roughly chopped
1 bunch of cilantro stems on, roughly chopped
4 sprigs of thyme
1 tablespoon dulse powder
1 tablespoon plus 1 teaspoon sea salt
16 cups water

Put all the ingredients in a large soup pot over high heat.

Bring to a boil, then reduce to medium-low heat and simmer for 2 hours.

Then remove from the heat and strain by pouring through a colander into a large bowl. Save the vegetables for a pureed soup if you like. Transfer the broth to glass mason jars and store, covered, in the refrigerator or freezer until you're ready to use.

LENTIL CURRY STEW

Makes 4-6 servings

While most of my soups are blended, this chunky stew is my favorite exception. It's easy, comforting, and nourishing. In fall when we're beginning to crave warm winter foods, or when we're still hanging onto the feeling of comfort food as spring begins, there's something about the combination of these flavors that I just can't get enough of. I love serving this family style, with bowls of chopped avocado, seeds, cilantro, and lime juice, so everyone can make their own bowl. For a really complete meal, I serve it with toasted buckwheat bread or soccas, red pepper cashew cream, and the simple green salad. I also save my veggie scraps for making broth later.

1 cup lentils, soaked for 30 minutes
4 cups vegetable broth
3 tablespoons coconut oil
4 cloves garlic, chopped
1 small yellow onion, diced
1 cup celery, diced
1 cup carrot, diced (1-2 large carrots)
1 bunch Swiss chard, chopped
1 head parsley, chopped
2 tablespoons red wine vinegar
2 teaspoons sea salt
1 teaspoon yellow curry powder
1 teaspoon cumin
1 teaspoon paprika
½ teaspoon ground black pepper
juice from ½ lemon (about 1 tablespoon)
Chopped avocado, cilantro, pumpkin seeds, and lime juice for the topping

Strain and rinse the lentils. Add the coconut oil, garlic, onion, carrots and celery, salt, and pepper to a medium-sized soup pot over high heat. Sauté for about 5 minutes, stirring a few times. Add the red wine vinegar, and stir for about 30 seconds.

Add the lentils, broth, curry powder, cumin, and paprika. Reduce the heat to medium and cook for another 15 minutes. Add the Swiss chard, parsley, and lemon juice, and cook for 5 more minutes.

Serve hot with your favorite toppings.

salads

As a young chef, working the salad station was one of the first times I had the freedom to be creative in a professional kitchen. Contrary to popular belief, I think salads are far from boring. They're so versatile! I love warm salads, raw salads, and salads where I get to combine raw and roasted ingredients. The Simple Green Salad is so light, while the Kale and Quinoa salad is a full-on meal. One day I'll have a cookbook just for salads, but for now, this chapter showcases a few of my favorites. You can sneak almost anything into a beautifully prepared salad, so feel free to get creative.

RAW CARROT BEET SALAD

Makes 4 servings

I love this salad when I am doing a light detox or cleanse because the vibrant raw vegetables make my body feel radiant. It's an especially helpful dish when I'm working on creating a more alkaline environment in my body, which is common for me. I'm always amazed at how much energy this salad gives me, and always confident that it's providing the raw enzymes I need for proper digestion. I love pairing this salad with a soup or an entrée for a well-rounded meal.

4 large carrots, peeled and grated
1 large beet, peeled and grated
juice from ½ lemon (about 1 tablespoon)
1 avocado, diced
2 tablespoons extra virgin olive oil
1 teaspoon sea salt
a handful of parsley leaves
a handful of activated pumpkin seeds

Put the carrot, beet, avocado, lemon, salt, and olive oil in a salad bowl.

Mix them all together using your hands until well combined, mashing the avocado with your fingers.

Fold in the parsley leaves and top with pumpkin seeds before serving.

SIMPLE GREEN SALAD

Makes 4 servings

I fell in love with this salad during my culinary training. It's so simple that I almost feel silly putting it in the book. But it's actually one of the salads that my friends ask for the most. Sometimes I think the simplicity is what makes it feel tricky. Each ingredient needs to be treated delicately to allow all the flavors to balance and shine. You'll get it right if you use my special technique for dressing this salad and use the same ratios every time. I believe there's no need to complicate salad dressings. All you need is an acid, salt, and a great quality olive oil. I eat this simple salad with most of my meals because it's so refreshing and easy to make.

1 bag mixed baby greens (about 6 cups)
a handful of mixed herbs (I use fennel fronds, mint, and parsley)
juice from 1 lemon (about 2 tablespoons)
½ teaspoon sea salt
¼ cup extra virgin olive oil

Combine the greens and herbs in a large salad bowl. Drizzle the lemon juice over the herbs and greens, then sprinkle the salt on top.

Carefully distribute the oil by pouring it along the inside rim of the bowl, all the way around so it can drip down into the bowl.

Gently toss the salad with your hands. Avoid over-mixing. Don't bruise those sexy greens!

STONE FRUIT SALAD

Makes 6 servings

When it's that special time in summer (which I call summer squash and stone fruit season,) this salad is my absolute favorite thing to serve. The combination of flavors is unbeatable. This unique summer salad goes perfectly with a glass of vinho verde, my favorite Portuguese wine. Please note this recipe should only be made in season. Subpar plums, peaches, and tomatoes would really make this salad fall flat.

1 pound of summer squash, sliced
1 pound of baby heirloom tomatoes, halved
4 plums, pitted, chopped into bite-size pieces, skin on
1 peach, pitted, chopped into bite-size pieces, skin on
¼ cup avocado oil or olive oil
1 teaspoon sea salt
½ cup pumpkin seed pesto (p. 107)
a handful of chopped herbs (I use cilantro, dill, mint, and fennel fronds)
a handful activated pumpkin seeds

Preheat the oven to 375 degrees and line two sheet pans with parchment paper.

In a small bowl, toss the squash with 2 tablespoons of oil, then spread the squash on the prepared sheet pan, and roast at 375 degrees for 20 minutes.

In the same bowl, toss the tomatoes with 2 tablespoons of oil, then spread on the second prepared sheet pan and roast at 375 degrees for 15 minutes.

Remove both pans and let them cool.

Combine the squash, tomatoes, plums, peaches, and salt in a large bowl. Use a spoon to gently toss them together, then fold in the fresh herbs.

Spread the pesto on a large platter. Then place the salad on top of the pesto and top with pumpkin seeds.

CREAMY KELP NOODLE SALAD

Makes 4-6 servings

2 (12-ounce) bags of kelp noodles
juice from ½ lemon (about 1 tablespoon)
1 teaspoon salt
1 ½ cups shiitake mushrooms, thinly sliced
½ cup carrot, julienned
4 bunches of scallions, thinly sliced, whites and greens (save a few pieces for garnish)
¼ cup basil, thinly sliced
12 mint leaves, torn
filtered water

ONION CASHEW CREAM

1 ¼ cups activated cashews
¾ cup water
2 tablespoons nutritional yeast
2 tablespoons diced red onion
2 teaspoons sumac
1 ½ teaspoons sea salt
½ teaspoon fresh ginger root, peeled
½ teaspoon fresh cracked black pepper
juice from ½ lemon (about 1 tablespoon)

Add the cashews and the rest of the ingredients for the cashew cream into a food processor or high-speed blender, and blend together until the mixture is a smooth cashew cream.

I don't think my luck gets better than seaweed shaped like pasta. There's so much you can do with kelp noodles, but this is my favorite way to use them. When I want to add more raw foods into my diet, this salad is such a gift. It's loaded with healthy fats, protein, and vitamins.
Eating raw foods doesn't have to feel restrictive. It can be fun, exciting, and an opportunity to get creative in the kitchen.

The easiest way to make this salad is to prepare the noodles, cashews, and mushrooms the night before, and assemble the salad with the raw ingredients the next day before serving.

Put the kelp noodles in a large bowl, add the lemon juice and salt, and cover with water. Use your fingers to break apart the clumps of noodles, and use food scissors to cut them into smaller, easier-to-eat pieces.

Cover the bowl and soak the noodles for at least an hour, but preferably overnight, refrigerated. You can soak your cashews and prepare the mushrooms the night before as well.

The next day, remove the mushrooms, kelp noodles, and cashews from the fridge. The mushrooms should have absorbed all the liquid and become tender. Set them aside. Strain the kelp noodles, discarding the liquid, and rinse well. Place the noodles in a large bowl.

Prepare the cashew cream and add it to the kelp noodles and use your hands to mix them together very well. All the noodles should be coated with cashew cream.
Add the mushrooms, carrots, scallions, and herbs, mixing to incorporate them into the cheesy noodles.

Salt to taste, and top with fresh cracked pepper and a few scallion slices for garnish.

MUSHROOM MARINADE

juice from 1 lemon (about 2 tablespoons)
1 tablespoon sherry vinegar

Place the thin mushroom slices in a shallow bowl or container and add the lemon juice and sherry vinegar. Let the mushrooms sit in the liquid for at least 5 minutes, but preferably overnight, covered, and refrigerated.

ROASTED BRUSSELS SPROUT SALAD

Makes 6 servings

I love the comforting nourishment of this warm salad. Searing the brussels sprouts allows them to caramelize, bringing out exceptional flavor. Their dark-golden caramelized color is lightened up by the bright pesto, so the color of this salad is earthy and beautiful. The combination of textures and the flavor of the pesto is what makes this dish a standout on any table.

2 pounds Brussels sprouts, halved with the ends cut off
3 tablespoons coconut oil
½ teaspoon sea salt
1 cup dried apricots or other dried fruit
½ cup roasted pistachios
1 cup pistachio pesto (p. 106)
a few cilantro leaves for garnish

Heat the coconut oil and Brussels sprouts in a large sauté pan over high heat. Cook for 8 minutes, stirring every few minutes to keep the sprouts from burning.

If the pesto isn't already made, you can make it while the Brussels sprouts are cooking.

Remove the Brussels sprouts from the heat. Transfer them to a bowl and add the pesto and dried fruit. Mix everything together so the pesto is well-incorporated and top with pistachios for a crunch. Serve warm.

QUINOA & KALE SALAD
WITH HERBS

Makes 4-6 servings

1 ½ cups quinoa
2 ¼ cups filtered water plus more for soaking
1 tablespoon lemon juice
½ teaspoon sea salt
1 cup cauliflower florets, cut into bite-sized pieces
¾ cup diced fennel
1 ½ teaspoons olive oil
¼ teaspoon sea salt
½ cup plus 2 tablespoons cashew cream (p. 108)
1 ½ cups Tuscan kale, de-stemmed and chopped
2 tablespoons cup chopped basil
2 tablespoons chopped mint
2 tablespoons chopped parsley
¾ cup radicchio, finely chopped
3 tablespoons activated pumpkin seeds
2 tablespoons fresh orange juice
1 tablespoon fresh lemon juice
¼ teaspoon crushed red pepper flakes
½ teaspoon sea salt
¼ teaspoon ground black pepper

Quinoa is one of those superfoods that really deserves the name. It has twice as much fiber as other grains and has all the essential amino acids to make a complete protein. That's because it's actually a seed, and not a grain at all. But it works quite well as a substitute for other grains like rice, orzo, or couscous. I like to incorporate it into salads, pilafs, and porridges to boost the nutrients in my meals. This is the hearty salad I make for every party because it's such a crowd-pleaser, and it ensures there's something on the table that I can eat. Everyone loves the creamy taste of the cashew cream, the bright flavor of the fresh herbs, and the crunch from the pumpkin seeds. This salad has the perfect balance of protein, healthy carbs, and vegetables to be a complete meal. It holds beautifully in the fridge, so if you're not feeding a group, you can keep small portions refrigerated to enjoy throughout the week.

Preheat the oven to 400 degrees and line a sheet pan with parchment paper.

Place the quinoa in a large bowl and cover it with water. Let it soak for 15 minutes.

While the quinoa is soaking, toss the cauliflower and fennel in a medium-sized bowl with the olive oil and salt. Spread them on the sheet pan and roast in the oven for 15-20 minutes until golden and tender. Remove the pan from the oven and let the veggies cool slightly.

Drain the quinoa, and place it in a pot with 2 ¼ cups water. Bring the quinoa and water to a boil over high heat, then reduce to low heat and cook, covered, for 15 minutes.

Remove the pot from the heat and let stand, covered, for 5 minutes before removing the lid and using a fork to fluff the quinoa. Gently stir in the lemon juice and salt, and set aside to cool slightly.

Whisk together the orange juice, lemon juice, salt, and pepper in a small bowl. Then add the cashew cream and whisk to combine.

Add the cashew cream dressing into the quinoa, mixing with a spoon to incorporate, then fold in the rest of the herbs and veggies. Serve immediately or refrigerate until ready to use.

NOTE about cooking quinoa:
Soaking your quinoa before you cook it will remove the bitter taste. I also like adding lemon and salt as soon as it's cooked so the little kernels soak up all that flavor and get very well-seasoned.

KALE SALAD
WITH CAULIFLOWER, BEET RADICCHIO

Makes 4-6 servings

1 large bunch of Tuscan kale, de-stemmed and torn
4 cups of cauliflower florets, cut into bite-sized pieces
1 small head of radicchio
1 small yellow beet, peeled, then shaved with a carrot peeler
8 pitted dates, sliced
½ cup chopped almonds
2 teaspoons ground turmeric
1 teaspoon paprika
1 cup plus 2 tablespoons extra virgin olive oil
½ teaspoon sea salt
¼ teaspoon ground black pepper
Juice from 1 lemon (about 2 tablespoons)
Juice from 1 orange (about 3 tablespoons)

DRESSING

¼ cup tahini
¾ cup extra virgin olive oil
2 tablespoons sherry vinegar
1 tablespoon lemon juice
½ teaspoon sea salt
¼ teaspoon ground black pepper

I have a theory that non-beet eaters are more likely to eat a yellow beet than a red beet, so I always choose yellow beets when serving large groups, or people I don't know. Test my theory, and see if you can get a beet-avoider to love this salad. The combination of warm, roasted vegetables with the raw shaved beets, massaged kale, sweet dates, and crunchy almonds make every bite interesting and delicious. This salad is great on its own, but it also complements fish or grilled meat very well. Tip: you can also blend this salad with some water or broth for a quick, nourishing soup.

Preheat the oven to 350 degrees. Prepare two sheet pans by lining them with parchment paper.

Combine the cauliflower, turmeric, ¼ cup olive oil, salt, pepper, paprika, and lemon in a bowl. Toss together until the cauliflower is coated. Then spread the cauliflower on one of the sheet pans. Roast for 30 minutes.

Thinly slice the radicchio and toss it in a mixing bowl with the orange juice, 2 tablespoons of olive oil, a pinch of salt, and a pinch of black pepper. Spread it on the second sheet pan and roast it for 8 minutes.

Once the cauliflower and radicchio are out of the oven, whisk the dressing ingredients together in a small bowl.

Add the kale to a salad bowl and massage ¼ cup of the dressing into the torn kale with your fingers for one to two minutes. Add the warm veggies, raw shaved beets, and dates to the bowl. Season with salt and pepper to taste, and top with almonds, adding more dressing if you like.

veggie mains & sides

These vegetable-based dishes work exceptionally well as sides paired with an entrée of your choice, or you can mix and match your favorites as shared small plates comprising a veggie-based meal. One of my favorite things to do with veggies is to use them unconventionally as a nutrient-dense substitute for grains like pasta or rice. My motto is: there's nothing you can't do with a vegetable!

ZUCCHINI NOODLES
WITH PESTO & TOMATO

Makes 4 servings

I love this versatile dish hot or cold, as a main or side, for lunch or dinner. As a side dish, it pairs well with a piece of grilled or seared salmon or cod. As a main dish, I accompany this with a simple green salad (p. 61) and for extra protein, I add a scoop of collagen powder to the pesto before mixing everything together.

1 tablespoon extra virgin olive oil
2 10-ounce containers of zucchini noodles or use a veggie spiralizer to make noodles from 4-5 large zucchinis
2 cups baby grape tomatoes, rinsed
½ cup pumpkin seed carrot top pesto (p. 107)
¼ cup activated pumpkin seeds
a pinch of sea salt
a pinch of ground black pepper
Optional: Almond Ricotta (p. 108) for topping

Heat the olive oil in a medium-sized sauté pan over medium-high heat. Add the tomatoes and cook for about five minutes until the skins start to blister and soften, careful not to burn them.

Add the noodles and cook for just 1 minute.

In a medium-sized bowl, combine the zucchini and tomato mixture with the pesto, salt, and pepper and mix until the noodles are coated.

Top with pumpkin seeds as you plate the noodles, and add big spoonfuls of almond ricotta if you like.

BUTTERNUT SQUASH, KALE, ONIONS, SEEDS & HERBS

Makes 4-6 servings

This is another staple in my house. I love eating this cold in salads, as a main meal or I will add some ground wild bison. Pair this with the zucchini noodles and a green salad for a complete meal!

¼ cup extra virgin olive oil
1 medium-sized butternut squash, peeled, deseeded, and cubed into ½ pieces*.
1 medium yellow onion, diced
1 medium fennel bulb, diced
1 bunch Tuscan kale, de-stemmed and roughly chopped
2 cups fresh spinach, roughly chopped
1 bunch of cilantro, roughly chopped
juice from 1 lemon (about 2 tablespoons)
2 teaspoons sea salt
1 teaspoon ground black pepper
Optional: ¼ cup activated sunflower seeds
¼ cup activated pumpkin seeds
¼ teaspoon crushed red pepper flakes for some heat

Preheat the oven to 375 degrees.

Combine the olive oil, onion, fennel, salt, and pepper in a large oven-safe sauté pan and sauté over medium heat for 15 minutes, stirring a few times, careful not to let the onion and fennel burn.

Add the squash and sauté for 10 minutes, stirring constantly until the squash begins to soften. Then add the kale, spinach and the lemon juice.

Put the whole pan in the oven and cook for 30 minutes at 375.

Carefully remove the pan when it's finished, and add the cilantro before dividing up into bowls. Top each bowl with a sprinkling of activated seeds, and some crushed red pepper flakes if you like it spicy.

*You can also buy pre-cut squash, but make sure the size is about ½ inch.

SPAGHETTI SQUASH CASSEROLE

Makes 6 servings

1 large spaghetti squash
3 roma tomatoes, diced
1 cup fresh spinach, chopped
¾ cup red pepper cashew cream
(p.107)
¼ cup plus 2 teaspoons extra virgin
olive oil
1 ½ teaspoons sea salt
6 basil leaves
Optional: ½ cup almond ricotta
(p.108)

ALMOND CRUMBLE

1 cup activated almonds
2 tablespoons nutritional yeast
1 teaspoon sea salt
1 teaspoon ground black pepper

Spaghetti squash is one of nature's amazing inventions. Its insides, once cooked, are naturally shaped like spaghetti. If you're craving spaghetti, but staying away from conventional pasta, it's a great grain-free option. It's high in fiber, folic acid, potassium, and beta-carotene. Even though I appreciate a good Italian pasta, I prefer this when I want more nutrition and less starch. I love this warm casserole because it's creamy, comforting, and delicious... and there's nothing in it that I ever regret eating.

Preheat oven to 400 degrees.

Cut the squash in half lengthwise and scrape out the seeds with a spoon. Spread a teaspoon of olive oil on the inside of each half. Place both halves on a baking sheet skin-side up. Bake for 45 minutes.

Blend the ingredients for the almond crumble in a food processor for one minute until finely ground, then transfer to a bowl and set aside.

When the squash is done, remove it from the oven and let it cool for 15-20 minutes. Once it's easy to touch without burning your fingers, scrape the insides (the "spaghetti") out with a fork into a large bowl. Discard the skins.

Add the rest of the ingredients to the large bowl and mix together well with a spoon.

Coat an 8x8 casserole or cake pan with coconut oil. Transfer the mixture into the pan and press it down to flatten it evenly. Sprinkle the almond crumble on top and bake for 25 minutes. Let cool for at least 15 minutes before serving.

POLENTA
WITH HEMP SEED OLIVE TAPENADE

Makes 6 servings

2 cups quick-cooking polenta
1 (13.5 ounce) can full-fat coconut milk
4 ½ cups filtered water
1 teaspoon sea salt
½ teaspoon ground black pepper
3 tablespoons plant-based butter
a small handful of chopped mixed herbs (whatever you have on hand, I usually use basil.)
½ cup sundried tomatoes, diced

HEMP SEED TAPENADE

2 cups castelvetrano olives, pitted**
1 garlic clove, peeled
½ cup parsley leaves
¼ cup hemp seeds
2 teaspoons capers
1 teaspoon ground black pepper
1 tablespoon lemon juice
½ cup olive oil

Hot or cold, this crowd-pleaser hasn't failed me yet. For years I've made this dish for parties and catering gigs, and it's always a hit. I love the versatility. If you don't love a tapenade, you could top this with red pepper cashew cream, pesto, or something else that tickles your fancy. Just enjoy!

Preheat the oven to 375 degrees. Lightly coat an 8-inch square casserole or cake pan with coconut oil.

In a medium-sized soup pot, bring the coconut milk and water to a boil. Add the polenta and stir constantly for 5 minutes until it becomes thick. Turn off the heat and add the rest of the ingredients. Mix together and pour into the prepared pan and bake for 30 minutes. Let it cool for about 30 minutes before cutting into small pieces. Top with the tapenade before serving.

For the tapenade:
Combine the olives, garlic cloves, parsley leaves, hemp seeds, capers, and black pepper in a food processor and pulse until finely chopped.

Scrape the mixture into a bowl and stir in the lemon juice and olive oil by hand until well incorporated.

Keep covered tightly, refrigerated, for up to five days.

NOTE about pitting olives:
The easiest way to pit olives without any special equipment is to use a large chef's knife. Place the olive under the flat side of the blade, and give it a good smack with the palm of your hand. This will smash the olive and allow you to pull out the pit easily. Be sure to arch your fingers up so they stay out of the way of the sharp side of the blade.

SOCCAS TWO WAYS

Makes 4-6 servings

1 cup chickpea flour
1 cup water
2 tablespoons olive oil
2 tablespoons chopped soft herbs
(parsley, chives, basil)
¾ teaspoon sea salt
¼ teaspoon ground cumin
⅛ teaspoon crushed red pepper
flakes (optional)
Olive oil or coconut oil for cooking

Soccas are a cross between a savory pancake and crepe made from chickpea flour. Get creative with these grain-free soccas, and use them for tostadas, tacos, or toasts. The batter does have to sit a while before frying, so you can make it ahead and fry up your soccas whenever you're ready.

Preheat the oven to 375 degrees. Lightly coat a 8-inch square casserole or cake pan with coconut oil.

Whisk all the ingredients together until smooth, and let the batter sit for at least an hour, letting the flour hydrate.

Heat a 6- or 8-inch skillet over medium heat. Once the pan is very hot, add 1 tablespoon of olive or coconut oil.

Spoon ¼ cup of batter into the pan, tilting the pan to distribute the batter evenly around the entire bottom of the pan. Once the batter covers the bottom of the pan, let it sit over medium heat until the socca begins to bubble and turn brown around the edges, about one minute. Use a spatula to flip the socca and cook the second side just 30 seconds before removing it from the pan.

MEDITERRANEAN STYLE

1 medium-sized fennel bulb, thinly sliced
¼ cup finely chopped parsley
1 tablespoon lemon juice
1 tablespoon olive oil
¼ teaspoon sea salt
1 ½ cups roasted beet and walnut hummus
(p. 109)
¾ cup of almond ricotta (p. 108)

Toss together the fennel, parsley, lemon juice, olive oil, and salt to create a slaw.

Prepare your soccas and then spread ¼ cup of hummus on each and top with the Mediterranean style slaw and some almond ricotta.

MEXICAN STYLE

2 cups shredded green cabbage
¼ cup finely chopped cilantro
2 radishes, thinly sliced
1 tablespoon lime juice
1 tablespoon olive oil
¼ teaspoon sea salt
1 ½ cups spicy black bean hummus (p. 109)
1 avocado, sliced

Begin by making your black bean hummus. Toss together the cabbage, cilantro, radish, lime juice, olive oil, and salt.

Prepare your soccas and then spread ¼ cup of hummus on each and top with Mexican style slaw and some sliced avocado.

TAHINI ROASTED CARROTS

Makes 4 servings

veggies & mains

I absolutely love this dish for its complex flavor profile. The dill, pistachios, and dates paired with the sweet, earthy carrots and the nutty, creamy tahini makes for a truly divine and unique experience. I love this dish warm or cold with a large green salad and some grilled salmon. It also presents beautifully on a big platter, so it's great for dinner parties.

About carrots: Rather than peeling my carrots, I soak them in some apple cider vinegar for about 10 minutes and then scrub them with a veggie brush and rinse them clean.

2 bunches carrots with their tops on (about 1 ½ pounds)
8 pitted dates, chopped
3 tablespoons pistachios, out of their shells, roasted, salted and chopped
2 tablespoons dill, chopped
2 tablespoons avocado oil or melted coconut oil

Orange Tahini Dressing:
juice from 2 oranges (about 6 tablespoons)
¼ cup tahini
¼ cup extra virgin olive oil
1 tablespoon sherry vinegar
¼ teaspoon sea salt

Preheat oven to 350 degrees.

Clean or peel the carrots and toss them with 2 tablespoons of avocado oil or melted coconut oil. Spread them on a baking sheet and roast them in the oven for 30 minutes.

Remove the carrots from the oven and let them cool while you prepare the dressing.

In a small bowl, whisk the tahini, olive oil, orange juice, vinegar, and salt until creamy, about one minute.

Once the carrots are cool, toss them with the dill and ¾ cup of the dressing. Place them on a big platter and top with the pistachios and the dates.

BROWNED RICE, PESTO, VEGGIES

Makes 4-6 servings

This rice was one of the first dishes my grandma taught me how to make, and the smell reminds me of her. It's my comfort food. I had to put my healthy spin on it, so I added a bunch of veggies, but my favorite way to eat it is plain.

3 cups water or broth
2 cups white basmati rice
2 cups raw kale, chopped
2 cups carrots, chopped into 1-inch pieces
2 cups sunchokes, chopped into 1-inch pieces
½ cup pumpkin seed carrot top pesto (p. 107)
¼ cup extra virgin olive oil
½ bunch of parsley, chopped
juice from 1 ½ lemons (about 3 tablespoons)
1 teaspoon sea salt
1 teaspoon ground black pepper

Preheat the oven to 350 degrees. Dry roast the chopped sunchokes and carrots (without any oil or seasoning) on a baking sheet in the oven for 30 minutes.

Prepare the pesto and place a medium-sized pot over high heat and add the oil and rice. Stir constantly, letting the rice brown but not burn, for about 5 minutes. Add the water or broth, reduce heat to low, and cover the pan. Cook on low for 15 minutes. Do not touch it while it's cooking!

When it's finished, stir in the kale, roasted veggies, and pesto. Add the salt, pepper, lemon juice, and parsley. Top each serving with a drizzle of olive oil and a handful of any favorite nuts or seeds.

YAM FRIES
WITH COCONUT AIOLI

Makes 2-3 servings

When I was doing a paleo autoimmune cleanse, I started eating these fries for a sweet and savory treat. I love yams as a paleo potato substitute.

1 large yam
¼ cup coconut oil, melted
2 teaspoons dried basil
1 teaspoon sea salt
½ teaspoon crushed red pepper flakes
¼ teaspoon paprika

Preheat the oven to 375 degrees.

Peel the yam. Cut it in half lengthwise and then into ½-inch wide fries, or thicker if you prefer.

Whisk the rest of the ingredients together to make a spiced coconut oil in a bowl large enough to fit the fries.

Toss the yam fries in the spiced coconut oil, and then lay them out evenly on a baking sheet.

Bake for 25-30 minutes until slightly crispy.

PARSNIP AND SWEET POTATO GRATIN

Makes 6 servings

CASSEROLE

2 cups chopped cauliflower
1 large sweet potato, thinly sliced
by hand or with a mandolin
1 large parsnip, peeled and thinly
sliced by hand or with a mandolin
½ medium-sized yellow onion,
thinly sliced
1 ½ cups vegetable broth
1 cup almond milk
1 tablespoon nutritional yeast
2 garlic cloves
3 tablespoons sage, chopped
2 tablespoons extra virgin olive oil
1 ¼ teaspoons sea salt
½ teaspoon ground black pepper
½ teaspoon paprika

CRUMBLE

1 cup almond flour
½ cup activated almonds, chopped
2 tablespoons nutritional yeast
2 tablespoons extra virgin olive oil
1 teaspoon sumac
¼ teaspoon mustard seed powder
4 sage leaves, chopped
A pinch of crushed red pepper
flakes

This is a healthier version of a classic French gratin without dairy or cheese, but with just as much creamy delicious flavor. Instead of potatoes, I fill this casserole with cauliflower, sweet potato, and parsnip. Instead of cream and cheese, I use almond milk and nutritional yeast. A nice crumble on top makes for wonderful texture and flavor.

Preheat the oven to 400 degrees.

Place the cauliflower, garlic, and vegetable broth in a medium-sized pot over high heat. Bring it to a boil, then cover and cook over low heat for 5 minutes. Then remove the pot from heat and let cool slightly while you prepare the crumble.

In a separate bowl, combine all the ingredients for the crumble together in a bowl, mixing with your hands.

Transfer the hot cauliflower, broth, and garlic into a food processor, and add the yeast, salt, pepper, olive oil, paprika, and almond milk. Process until the mixture is creamy.

In a separate bowl, combine the potato, parsnip, sage, and onion with the cauliflower cream. Toss together until the vegetables are all coated in the cream.

Spray a 9x9 casserole pan lightly with coconut oil. Transfer the vegetables coated with cauliflower cream into the pan. Sprinkle the crumble evenly on top, and bake, covered, for 45 minutes. Then remove the cover and cook for 30 minutes until golden brown.

BROCCOLI RICE

Makes 4 servings

1 container broccoli rice, fresh or frozen (1 pound or about 4 cups)
2 packed cups fresh chopped spinach
1 cup coconut milk
1 bunch of parsley, chopped
1 bunch of cilantro, chopped
1 large red onion, finely chopped
3 tablespoons avocado oil or melted coconut oil
4 cloves garlic, minced
juice from 1 lemon (about 2 tablespoons)
2 ¼ teaspoons sea salt
1 teaspoon mustard seed powder
1 teaspoon dulse powder
1 teaspoon paprika
1 teaspoon sumac
½ teaspoon ground black pepper
juice from 1 lime (about 1 tablespoon)

I serve with:
1 avocado, peeled and sliced
¼ cup activated pumpkin seeds

Many veggie enthusiasts have fallen in love with substituting cauliflower rice for conventional rice. I love cauliflower rice, but I'm even more in love with broccoli rice! I make it during my weekly meal prep. It's great hot or cold, and when I want extra protein, I'll add some sardines on top. It's a great complement to a fish or meat entrée, too. If you're not sure where or when to use this, just use it in place of rice. There's quite a bit of cilantro in this recipe, which helps remove heavy metals from the body. With so many vitamins and nutrients in this broccoli rice, it's a valuable dish to add to the table.

Heat the oil and onion in a medium-sized soup pot over medium heat for 5 minutes to soften the onion. Then add the garlic, salt, pepper, and mustard seed powder and cook for 10 more minutes. Stir often so the spices don't burn.

Add the broccoli rice, stirring to coat, and sauté for 1 minute.

Add the coconut milk, spinach, lemon, paprika, sumac, and dulse. Stir to combine, and cook, covered, for 8 minutes. Remove the pan from the heat and stir in the chopped herbs and lime juice.

Serve in bowls topped with sliced avocado and activated pumpkin seeds.

WHY MUSTARD SEED POWDER?

Mustard seed powder helps our bodies to properly absorb the enzymes in cruciferous vegetables, so I try to use at least a pinch of mustard seed powder anytime I cook broccoli or cauliflower. I always want to get the maximum benefits from the food I put into my body.

bison & fish

I often get asked about my diet. Am I paleo, vegan, keto? Here's my answer: I eat a primarily plant-based diet, using meat as an accompaniment. When I serve myself a meal, I make sure that the majority of my plate is cooked and raw vegetables, and then I add my meat or fish. My diet usually ends up resembling a paleo diet because that is what has been feeling best for my body. Dairy and poultry no longer feel good in my body, while I feel great eating eggs, sustainable wild fish, and grass-fed wild bison.

I am picky about my protein because it matters to me how I feel, how I function, and the impact I make in the world. Choosing a company to supply your meat is an important task, and I've spent a good amount of time researching, contacting companies, and making sure I'm comfortable with my choices.

Wild Idea Buffalo is a company I love that has a beautiful farm and treats their bison with respect. Bison is a great alternative to beef because it's not over-farmed, it's easier to digest, and it's a low-cholesterol food with as many omega-3 fatty acids as salmon.

When it comes to fish, it's all about balance. I choose to only eat wild, sustainable fish and am careful not to over-eat the larger fish that have higher levels of mercury content.

I have learned that my body feels better when I eat some animal protein, so I find ways to incorporate it into my diet. Everybody is different, and I encourage you to work with a nutritionist if you are struggling to figure out which foods suit you best.

SEARED SALMON
WITH JOB'S TEARS, KALE AND ANCHOVIES

Makes 4 servings

SALMON

4 6-ounce salmon fillets (skin on
or off)
¼ cup chopped parsley
2 tablespoons avocado oil
½ teaspoon sea salt
¼ teaspoon ground black pepper
1 lemon

JOB'S TEARS

½ pound or 1 ½ cups Job's Tears
1 bunch Tuscan kale,
   de-stemmed and finely chopped
2 cups filtered water
3 oil-packed anchovy fillets
2 tablespoons red wine vinegar
2 tablespoons olive oil, divided
2 tablespoons plant-based butter
2 garlic cloves, minced
¾ teaspoon sea salt
¼ teaspoon ground black pepper

As a young chef, it would sometimes catch me by surprise when I would stumble upon a new ingredient. As a seasoned chef, I know there are worlds I don't know, and I welcome the discovery of new ingredients or new ways to use old ingredients. Being creative means that one piece of new information (like a new ingredient or technique) opens up whole worlds of possibility. That's what my journey as a chef who loves health and nutrition has been like. New worlds open to me constantly, and it's all I can do to live a normal-ish life and not be in a kitchen creating 24 hours a day!

Job's Tears was one of those new discoveries that excited me. It's a gluten-free grain also known as Chinese Barley, and it has a nice nutty flavor and the chewy texture of barley. I love it in this recipe with the anchovies, kale, and salmon, and I think you will, too. Try substituting Job's Tears for faro, brown rice, or barley in any recipe.

Job's Tears: Place the Job's Tears in a medium-sized pot and add enough water that there are at least 3-inches of water on top. Bring it to boil over high heat, then reduce the heat and simmer for 40 minutes or until tender. Drain the job's tears and dump them into a bowl. While warm, add the vinegar, salt, pepper, and 1 tablespoon olive oil. Stir to combine and set aside.
In a separate pot, bring 2 cups of water to a boil. Add a generous pinch of salt and add the chopped kale. Blanche for just 30 seconds, then drain and rinse under cold water. Press the kale into the strainer to remove any excess water. Set the kale aside.

Heat a large skillet over medium heat. Add the butter and 1 tablespoon of olive oil, then add the garlic and anchovies. Cook, mashing the anchovies, for 3-4 minutes until the anchovies are melted.

Add the kale to the skillet, and cook for just one minute, tossing the kale in the butter mixture. Remove the pan from the heat, stir in the Job's Tears, and taste. Adjust with more salt or pepper as needed.

Salmon: Remove salmon from the fridge 20 minutes before cooking and pat until very dry with a paper or cloth towel. Sprinkle salt and pepper on both sides of the salmon.

Heat a large skillet over high heat. Add the grapeseed oil. Add the salmon once the pan is very hot and let it sear, undisturbed, for 2-3 minutes on the first side. Flip with a spatula, and cook 2-3 minutes on the second side. Remove from the pan and pat off any excess oil.
Reheat the Job's Tears over medium heat briefly if needed.

Serve salmon on top of the Job's Tears. Finish with a squeeze of fresh lemon juice, a drizzle of olive oil, and some chopped parsley.

SALMON DIP
WITH ALMOND AIOLI

Makes 4-6 servings

Canned wild salmon makes this a super fast appetizer to prepare. This is the dip I make for Superbowl parties and catering events that's dairy-free and egg-free. I love this on a charcuterie board, on wraps or sandwiches, or served with the almond crackers.

One 18-ounce can of wild salmon*
(or salmon that has been cooked and cooled)
1 cup sliced almonds
½ cup water
¼ cup olive oil
2 scallions, diced
½ bunch parsley, chopped roughly
juice from 1 lemon (about 2 tablespoons)
juice from ½ orange (about 1 ½ tablespoons)
1 teaspoon sherry vinegar
1 teaspoon sea salt
½ teaspoon sumac or paprika
¼ teaspoon (or more) crushed red pepper flakes
Extra olive oil to garnish

Almond Aioli: In a blender, combine the almonds, water, oil, lemon and orange juice, vinegar, salt, pepper, sumac/paprika, and blend until creamy, about one minute, scraping the sides as you go.
Transfer the almond puree to a bowl and add the salmon, smashing them together with a spoon. The consistency should be similar to tuna salad.

Fold in the scallions and parsley. When you're ready to serve, garnish with a nice drizzle of extra virgin olive oil, some more chopped scallions, and some parsley leaves.

*Canned salmon can have bones, scales, and skin. Look for a can that says it has no bones or skin. Always pull out bones if you see them.

CHEESY ALMOND CRACKERS

Makes 6-8 servings

I love these homemade almond crackers with pumpkin seed pesto, cashew cream, or the salmon dip. I enjoy the rustic look of these crackers, broken from the pan, on a charcuterie board. They're high in protein and a good snack to keep me going throughout the day, so I often take them with me for sustenance on the go. They freeze well, so I even put them in my suitcase frozen and take them across the country with me, so I have what I need, wherever I am.

3 cups raw whole almonds, soaked overnight, strained, rinsed
¼ cup plus 2 tablespoons nutritional yeast
2 tablespoons arrowroot
2 tablespoons coconut oil
1 tablespoon fresh oregano leaves, chopped roughly
1 teaspoon sea salt
1 teaspoon minced garlic (about 3 cloves)
½ teaspoon sumac
½ teaspoon ground black pepper
¼ teaspoon crushed red pepper flakes

Preheat the oven to 350 degrees.

Blend the almonds in a food processor for 2 minutes, scraping the sides as you go.

Remove the ground almonds and put them in a medium-sized bowl.
Add the rest of the ingredients into the bowl and mix together with your hands until a dough forms.

Place the dough on a parchment-lined baking sheet. Flatten the dough with your hands or the back of a measuring cup to about ½-inch thick.

Bake the flattened dough for 28 minutes until it's a light golden brown, and then remove to let it cool. Cool for 15-20 minutes, then break into large crackers. Store leftover crackers in the fridge in an airtight container.

STEAMED COD
WITH HERBED CAULIFLOWER RICE

Makes 4 servings

1 head cauliflower or 4 cups riced cauliflower
2 cups frozen green peas
¾ cup bone broth or veggie broth
juice from 2 lemons (3 tablespoons for cooking and ½ lemon for finishing)
2 tablespoons coconut oil
2 tablespoons coconut butter
1 tablespoon nutritional yeast
¾ teaspoon sea salt
1/2 teaspoon ground black pepper
2 sprigs thyme leaves
1 tablespoon oregano leaves
4 5-ounce fillets of wild Alaskan Cod, with 1/4 cup water, 1/2 lemon, pinch
½ cup roasted pecans
½ lemon for garnish

I have been teaching this dish at cooking classes since the very beginning. The thyme, pecans, and coconut butter are some of my favorite special touches on this dish. If you want to use another fish, or cook regular rice instead of cauliflower rice, go for it! Make it your own and enjoy every bite.

Cauliflower: If you're starting with a head of cauliflower, rice it by cutting it in half, removing stem and leaves, chopping it into medium-sized pieces, and pulsing it in a food processor until it looks like rice.

Add the coconut oil and cauliflower rice in a medium-sized sauté pan. Sauté for 2 minutes over medium heat, stirring constantly.

Then add the peas, broth, salt, pepper, thyme, and oregano leaves. Cover and cook for 10 minutes. Remove the cover and add 2 tablespoons of lemon juice, the coconut butter, and nutritional yeast.

Cod: Bring ¼ cup water, a pinch of salt, and the remaining tablespoon of lemon juice to a light simmer in a medium-sized sauté pan over high heat. Add the 4 filets of cod, and cover. Reduce the heat to medium, and cook for 4 minutes. Then flip the filets, and cook 3-4 minutes on the second side until they're done and the fish starts to flake apart.

Remove the filets and squeeze lemon juice from the ½ lemon over all four.

Scoop a portion of cauliflower rice on each plate, and place the filet on top. Finish with a drizzle of olive oil and some chopped pecans.

ROASTED SEA BASS
WITH SALSA VERDE

Makes 4 servings

4 6-ounce sea bass filets, skin on
2 tablespoons avocado oil
a pinch of salt and pepper
1 cup parsley, chopped (save a few
parsley leaves for garnish)
½ cup extra virgin olive oil
¼ cup capers, chopped
1 tablespoon red wine vinegar
1 ½ teaspoons lemon juice
1 ½ teaspoons grated garlic
1 ½ teaspoons fresh oregano
leaves
1 teaspoon lemon zest
1 teaspoon fresh thyme leaves
½ teaspoon crushed red pepper
flakes
extra olive oil and sumac for
finishing

I love wild sea bass with the skin on. If wild snapper is easily available, you could use it in this recipe if you prefer it to sea bass. Ask your fishmonger to scale and gut your fish so you can have beautiful, clean, skin-on pieces. I love this dish because of its simplicity. The salsa verde is the perfect complement to this roasted fish, but it's also great as a dip or on avocado toast. Use it to dress up any simple meat, fish, or veggie dish. It really shines when you have a beautiful great quality extra virgin olive oil.

Preheat the oven to 425 degrees and let the fish sit out for 30 minutes so it can reach room temperature. Lightly salt and pepper both sides of each filet.

Mix all the ingredients for the salsa verde together in a small mixing bowl and set aside.

Put a cast iron (or oven-safe) pan over high heat. Once the pan is hot, add the avocado oil. Place the fish in the pan, skin side down, and let it sear for 2 minutes. Flip each piece to sear for two more minutes on the other side. Carefully remove the pan from the heat and put it in the oven for 5 minutes, letting the skin brown.

Remove the pan from the oven and drizzle some extra virgin olive oil and a big spoonful of salsa verde. Finish with a sprinkle of sumac. Garnish each plate with some big fresh parsley leaves.

EVERYONE'S FAVORITE BISON SAUTÉ

Makes 4 servings

1 pound wild bison
1 bunch Tuscan kale, roughly chopped
4 roma tomatoes, roughly chopped
1 small red onion, finely diced
½ bunch parsley, finely diced
½ bunch cilantro, finely diced
¼ cup avocado oil
4 cloves garlic, diced
juice from 1½ lemons (about 3 tablespoons)
2 tablespoons fresh turmeric, peeled, finely diced
2 tablespoons fresh ginger, peeled, finely diced
1½ teaspoon salt
1 teaspoon dulse powder
¾ teaspoon black pepper

This is my go-to meal to make for friends, and it's almost always a part of my Sunday meal prep. It's delicious as a hot meal, but I also love eating leftovers cold, on top of a green salad. My favorite part of this dish is the bit you get from the fresh ginger and turmeric. If I don't have kale or the right herbs on hand, I'll use whatever greens I have in the fridge that need to get used up. I've used spinach, dandelion greens, and any herb you can think of. It always turns out exquisite. As always, I encourage you to get creative, and not to overthink it. See what kind of kitchen magic you can make.

1 pound wild bison
1 bunch Tuscan kale, roughly chopped
4 roma tomatoes, roughly chopped
1 small red onion, finely diced
½ bunch parsley, finely diced
½ bunch cilantro, finely diced
¼ cup avocado oil
4 cloves garlic, diced
juice from 1½ lemons (about 3 tablespoons)
2 tablespoons fresh turmeric root, peeled, finely diced
2 tablespoons fresh ginger root, peeled, finely diced
1½ teaspoon sea salt
1 teaspoon dulse powder
¾ teaspoon ground black pepper

Add the oil, onion, garlic, salt, and pepper to a large sauté pan over medium heat, and sauté for 10 minutes, stirring occasionally.

Then add the tomatoes, turmeric, and ginger, and sauté for 2 minutes before adding the bison. Break the bison apart in the pan with your spatula. Let the bison cook in the pan, broken apart, about 2 minutes before adding the kale, lemon, and dulse.

Cover the pan and let cook for 8 minutes. Then turn off the heat and add the herbs.
Serve hot with a simple green salad (p. 61) or with broccoli rice.

SALT & ACID

To make any sauté dish delicious, you just need a little salt and a little acid. Fresh lemon juice is my acid of choice. I used to think I had to have fancy wines and vinegars, but a good juicy lemon does the trick! Sherry vinegar and red wine vinegar are my favorite vinegars to keep on hand, and I will use vinegar as my acid if I don't have a lemon ready.

MY FAVORITE BLACK COD

Makes 4 servings

4 6-ounce wild black cod filets, skin on
½ butternut squash, peeled, diced into ½ inch pieces
1 bunch Tuscan kale, de-stemmed and chopped
1 bunch parsley, chopped
2 teaspoons avocado oil for searing
1 small yellow onion, diced
6 garlic cloves, diced
3 tablespoons coconut oil
juice from 2 lemons (3 tablespoons for cooking and ½ lemon for finishing)
2 tablespoons coconut aminos
1 ½ teaspoons sea salt
¼ teaspoon crushed red pepper flakes
olive oil for finishing

As soon as I can get wild black cod fresh in season, I rush to make this dish, and my friends and family rejoice. You can definitely substitute wild atlantic cod, snapper, or salmon. The butternut squash and kale that accompanies this cod is another favorite veggie combo of mine, and I make extra during meal prep so I can add it (hot or cold) to my wraps and salads.

Preheat the oven to 400 degrees and remove the cod from the fridge. Pat the filets dry with a paper towel, and sprinkle salt and pepper on both sides, letting them sit out while you prepare the kale and squash.

Add the oil, onion, garlic, salt, and pepper to a medium-sized oven-safe sauté pan over medium heat and sauté for 10 minutes. Add the squash and sauté another 10 minutes, stirring constantly. Then add the kale and the lemon, and transfer the pan from the stovetop to the preheated oven to roast for 20 minutes.

When you have 5 minutes left on the timer, put a large oven-safe skillet on high heat. When the timer goes off, remove the squash and kale from the oven and set aside. Turn the oven heat up to a high broil.

Add the avocado oil to the skillet and let the pan get very hot. Then place the cod filets skin side down with at least and inch between them, and let them sear about 3 minutes, undisturbed, until golden brown. Flip with a spatula and sear on the second side for 3 minutes.

Pour the coconut aminos and lemon juice over the filets and put both pans in the oven to roast for 5 minutes until the cod is golden brown and flaky. After 5 minutes, remove both pans from the oven and remove the bones from the fish if you haven't already. Serve each filet on top of a bed of squash and kale. Finish with a drizzle of olive oil and a squeeze of fresh lemon juice.

DEBONING FISH

See if your fishmonger can remove the bones for you. Black cod has a lot of bones. If I'm cooking for friends or family, I try to make sure everything's removed ahead of time. If I'm just cooking for myself, I will remove the bones with tweezers when the fish is just out of the oven, because it's easier when the fish is hot.

BISON BURGER

Makes 4 servings

BURGER

1 pound ground wild bison
2 tablespoons sherry vinegar
1 teaspoon sumac
1 teaspoon cumin
¾ teaspoon sea salt
¾ teaspoon ground black pepper
½ teaspoon ground ginger
1 tablespoon avocado oil for the pan

PICKLED ONION

2 red onions, thinly sliced
juice from 2 lemons (about 4 tablespoons)
1 tablespoon apple cider vinegar
¼ teaspoon sea salt

ACCOUTREMENTS (FOR EACH BURGER)

Oat Seed Roll (p. 47)
1 tablespoon egg aioli (p. 105)
1 tablespoon Pumpkin Seed Carrot Top Pesto (p. 107)
1 avocado, sliced
4 large lettuce leaves
4 slices of tomato if tomatoes are in season

If you're nervous about trying bison instead of beef for your burger, don't worry! You won't even notice the difference. I always use bison and my guests have no idea until I tell them. This is my favorite burger because I make every component of this burger with love and I know it is nourishing my body. How often do you have a burger that you know is so good for you?

The pickled onions (best made the night before, but at least an hour before serving) are great to have around because they're a fun topping for salads, great in sandwiches, wraps, toasts, and roasted veggies. Skip the tomato on top of this burger if tomatoes are out of season. In my opinion, there is nothing worse than an unripe tomato.

For well-done burgers, preheat the oven to 400 degrees.

Add the burger ingredients (except the oil) to a large mixing bowl, and mash everything together with your hands. When the mixture is nicely mashed, form it into 4 patties and heat the oil in a skillet over high heat.

Sear the burgers in the hot pan for 3 minutes on each side. If you want your burgers more well-done, finish them in a 400-degree oven for 5 minutes.

Slice the oat seed rolls in half like a bun, and spread coconut aioli on one side, and pesto on the other. Place the burger on top of the aioli and top with lettuce, avocado, and pickled red onion. If tomatoes are in season, add a slice of a sexy ripe tomato.

Pickled Onion:
Combine the onions, lemon juice, salt, and vinegar in an airtight jar in the fridge to let the onions pickle.

BISON BOLOGNESE
WITH ZUCCHINI NOODLES

Makes 2-3 servings

1 pound ground wild bison
2 large carrots, peeled
2 celery stalks
1 small yellow onion
¼ cup olive oil
4 garlic cloves, peeled and chopped
1 28-ounce can San Marzano tomatoes, mashed with your hands
1 ½ teaspoons sea salt
1 teaspoon ground black pepper
2 sprigs of fresh thyme
2 bay leaves
1/8 teaspoon ground cinnamon
1 ½ tablespoons red wine vinegar
a handful of parsley leaves, chopped
6 cups zucchini noodles

If you're not quite ready to embrace zucchini noodles, you can make this with traditional pasta. You might even enjoy this bolognese sauce over rice. But zucchini noodles curb my carb craving, and I love this as a low-carb, paleo take on a traditional Italian meal. I've had a lot of luck winning over veggie-noodle-resistant eaters with this dish.

Either finely dice the carrots, celery, and onion, or add them to a food processor and pulse until chopped into small pieces. Add the carrots, celery, onion, garlic, and oil in a medium-sized soup pot over medium heat. Sauté for 10 minutes. Then add the bison, and cook for 3 minutes, breaking the meat apart into smaller chunks with a spatula.

Then add the rest of the ingredients except for the parsley. (Make sure you've mashed those tomatoes before they go into the pot!)

Turn the heat down to medium-low, cover the pot, and cook for 20 minutes. Remove the bay leaves thyme sprigs.

If you're serving 4 people, add all the zucchini noodles into the pot and stir for 2 minutes before removing the pot from the heat. Divide into 4 bowls and top with a drizzle of olive oil and the parsley.

If you're just serving one person, for now, remove the sauce from the heat and put 1½ cups of zucchini noodles and 1 cup of the sauce into a small sauté pan over medium-low heat. Cook for two minutes, stirring to coat the noodles with the sauce. Remove from heat and serve, topped with a drizzle of olive oil a sprinkle of parsley leaves.

Truth be told, I love to snack, and I love sweets. I'm always excited to find ways to create sweets and snacks that actually nourish me and don't involve a sugar high followed by a crash. After spending years snacking on all the wrong foods, I have learned to add snacks and sweets into my Sunday meal prep, setting myself up for success by making healthy snacks I can enjoy all week long. My formula for a "healthy" treat is one that is high in protein, fat and fiber, and low in sugar. You should be able to enjoy everything in this chapter (including the more decadent desserts) guilt-free, knowing you are truly nourishing your body. I never want to feel guilty or deprived, which means I have to get creative. Let's take the guilt out of sweet treats by finding ways to enjoy our favorites while remaining aligned, confident, and strong in our bodies.

snacks & sweets

PALEO GRANOLA BAR

Makes 10 pieces

Non-Stick Cooking Spray (I like coconut oil)
2 cups almond flour
1 cup unsweetened shredded coconut
1 cup raw sunflower seeds
1 cup raw pecans
½ cup raw sliced or slivered almonds
½ cup pitted dates, diced
½ cup melted coconut oil
¼ cup maple syrup
2 tablespoons filtered water
2 teaspoons vanilla extract
½ teaspoon sea salt

I love granola bars, but most of the ones you find at the store are sneakily unhealthy. They all look like they're super clean, but many have ingredients you'd never think to eat, and they're so processed! You know I like real, whole, foods, so I had to make my own granola bars. When I make my own, I know I am fueling my body with nourishing food it needs and can use. These bars are loaded with protein, healthy fats, and fiber. I eat them for breakfast or a snack. To turn them into desert, I will take a piece still warm from the oven (or heated) and top it with banana ice cream (p. 102). Healthy ice cream sandwich, anyone?

Preheat the oven to 350 degrees and place the rack in the top third of the oven.

Line a 9 ½ " x 13" sheet pan with parchment paper. Spray the edges of the pan with non-stick spray.

In a food processor, combine the coconut, sunflower seeds, pecans, and almonds. Pulse until finely chopped for about 1 minute.

Add the almond flour and sea salt and pulse 2-3 more times.

Then add the coconut oil, maple syrup, water, dates, and vanilla. Process until the mixture becomes dough-like, and begins to pull away from the sides of the bowl.

Dump the mixture into the prepared pan and press it evenly and firmly to the edges. You can wet your hands to make it easier. You can also use a mallet or the back of a measuring cup to press down and even out the dough.

Bake for 10 minutes, then rotate the pan and bake another 6 minutes until lightly golden on top and darker golden around the edges.

Remove the pan and let cool completely, for at least 15 minutes.

Cut into bars in the size you like, and store in an air-tight container, for up to a week. These also freeze great!

SWEET POTATO
OR PUMPKIN BITES

Makes 16 pieces

1 ½ cups canned sweet potato puree or pumpkin puree
½ cup vanilla pea protein powder
3 tablespoons softened coconut butter*
1 tablespoon granulated monk fruit sweetener
1 teaspoon ground cinnamon
¼ teaspoon nutmeg
¼ teaspoon ground cloves
a pinch of sea salt
2 tablespoons cacao nibs for topping

Or substitute: unsweetened shredded coconut, chopped nuts, chocolate chips, pumpkin seeds, or dried blueberries

These bites are ready in less than 10 minutes and are a perfect post-workout or lunchbox snack because they have high protein and no added sugar at all. You can get creative and add dried fruit, chocolate chips, or seeds instead of the cacao nibs if you like. I've listed a few of my favorite substitutions below. I make these all year round with sweet potato, but I substitute pumpkin when it's fall and we want all things pumpkin! If you prefer to make your own puree, just roast a whole sweet potato at 400 degrees for 35 minutes, then when cool, peel with your fingers and puree in a blender.

Whisk the sweet potato or pumpkin puree and coconut butter together in a small bowl.

Add the rest of the ingredients and whisk until smooth.

Roll the dough into small balls with your hands, about the size of golf balls.

Roll the balls into the cacao nibs or other fun topping.

Chill before eating. Store in the refrigerator or the freezer to defrost when ready. These will last 3 months in the freezer.

*To soften coconut butter, put a little in a glass bowl in a warm oven for 5 minutes.

BLUE MAJIK POWER BALLS

Makes 24 pieces

These bites are another favorite at The Source Cafe. If you can't tell by now, I love rolling everything into balls. It makes for a treat that's easy to eat on the go. These blue balls are popular because of their high protein, fat, and fiber, low carbs, and no sugar. Amazingly, they taste like cookie dough! Blue Majik is an algae product sold by E3Live that boasts incredible muscle recovery in addition to all the benefits of algae – without the algae flavor.

Dry Ingredients:
2 cups almond flour
¼ cup collagen powder
¼ cup monk fruit powder
2 teaspoons ground cinnamon
1 teaspoon Blue Majik

Wet Ingredients:
1 "flax egg" (Mix 3 tablespoons water with 1 tablespoon flax meal and let sit 15 minutes.)
¼ cup coconut oil, melted
¼ cup softened coconut butter*
1 teaspoon vanilla extract

Mix together all the wet ingredients in a medium-sized bowl until creamy.

Add the dry ingredients into the bowl and mix with your hands until a thick dough forms.

Roll small portions into balls, the size of golf balls, and put them in the fridge for at least an hour. These are also great frozen and can be defrosted for an on-the-go snack.

Variation: GREEN MATCHA BALLS
Substitute 1 teaspoon matcha powder for the Blue Majik. Add ½ teaspoon spirulina.

*To soften coconut butter, put a little in a glass bowl in a warm oven for 5 minutes.

OAT BLUEBERRY BITES

Makes 24 pieces

2 cups gluten-free oats
2 cups almond butter (store-bought or using the recipe below)
1 cup dried blueberries (unsweetened)
²/₃ cup maple syrup
¾ cup hemp seeds
6 tablespoons vanilla pea protein powder
2 tablespoons chia seeds
1 tablespoon maca powder
1 teaspoon ground cinnamon
1 teaspoon sea salt

HOMEMADE ALMOND BUTTER

Makes 3 ½ cups

3 cups activated raw almonds
a pinch of sea salt

Popular at The Source Cafe as a pre-and post-workout snack as well as a lunchbox treat and car snack, these bites are a hit with every member of the family. Bonus: you can sneak adaptogens or matcha into these without detecting the taste. I've been known to add chocolate chips in, or substitute them for the berries when making these for my nephews.

Combine all of the ingredients in a medium-sized bowl and mash them all together with your hands until the dough is uniform. Roll small portions into golf balls, and enjoy! Store in the fridge or freezer.

Making your own almond butter is really quite easy, just takes some time and patience. If your almonds are already activated, it will save you some time.

Blend the almonds and salt in a food processor for 15-18 minutes, scraping the sides every 2 minutes. If you're patient, it will eventually turn into creamy almond butter.

Note: If you are using a high-speed blender instead of a food processor, or if you are using raw almonds that are not activated, add 3 tablespoons of olive oil to speed the process along.

ZUCCHINI BROWNIES
WITH TAHINI FROSTING

Makes 10 pieces

I love brownies, but I don't love the sugar, dairy, or eggs that they traditionally call for. These brownies are loaded with fiber, healthy fats, omega 3 fatty acids, and protein. And there's no call for guilt here because the base of these brownies is zucchini! If you prefer, you can substitute cauliflower or sweet potato for the zucchini. Great way to sneak in your veggies, right? Enjoy these guilt-free, sugar-free, dairy-free, vegan, paleo, keto brownies!

1 cup vanilla pea protein powder
2 large zucchini, ends discarded, roughly chopped into small pieces
½ cup raw cacao powder
1 tablespoon maca powder
1 teaspoon ground cinnamon
1 teaspoon baking soda
1 teaspoon baking powder
a pinch of sea salt
1 "flax egg"
mix 1 tablespoon flax with and 3 tablespoons water and let sit 15 minutes
Optional: 1 teaspoon of your favorite adaptogen. (I like lion's mane, reishi, and ashwagandha)

For the frosting:
¼ cup plus 1 tablespoon tahini
¼ cup plus 1 tablespoon vanilla pea protein powder
¼ cup monk fruit powder
¼ cup plus 2 tablespoons water, or more for a thinner frosting

Preheat the oven to 350 degrees and spray small muffin tins with coconut oil.
In a high-speed blender or food processor, puree 2 large zucchini to get 1 1/2 cups of zucchini puree.

Add all of the rest of the ingredients and blend until smooth.

Scoop the batter into small muffin tins and bake for 12 minutes. Let cool before enjoying.
You can also prepare these as larger muffins or in a cake pan, but they'll need to bake longer.

Whisk together all the ingredients for the frosting in a bowl. Place a large dollop on top of each muffin. Save any extra for toasts or dipping apple slices.

SPICED YAM "FLAN"

Makes 8 servings

non-stick cooking spray (I like coconut oil)
1 medium yam, peeled, diced into 1-inch cubes
2 cups full-fat coconut milk
6 tablespoons vanilla pea protein powder
1 teaspoon ground cinnamon
¼ teaspoon sea salt
4 drops stevia
5 extra-large eggs

Optional toppings:
whipped coconut cream
toasted pumpkin seeds
ground cinnamon
toasted unsweetened shredded coconut
cacao nibs
toasted pecans
sautéed apples

Don't you agree that the best food tastes good, feels good, and nourishes you? I love this take on Mexican flan made from pureed roasted yams because it checks everything on the list. It's sweet without refined sugar, rich without dairy, and unexpectedly nourishes you with protein. It makes a beautiful dessert topped with whipped coconut cream and cacao nibs, but I eat it as a snack at any time of day. Note: you can use another nut milk, but coconut milk makes this dessert perfectly creamy.

Preheat the oven to 375 degrees.

Spray 8 6-ounce ramekins OR an 8-inch square baking dish with non-stick cooking spray. Place the diced yam on a small baking sheet and dry roast it (with no oil or seasoning) for 20 minutes or until fork-tender. Remove and let cool slightly.

Reduce oven heat to 350 degrees.

Measure out 1 cup of the roasted yams. Store any remaining yams for future use – I like to freeze them to use in the refueler smoothie (p. 25).

In a high-speed blender, combine the 1 cup roasted yam, coconut water, diluted coconut milk, protein powder, cinnamon, salt, and stevia. Blend until very smooth.

Add the eggs and pulse briefly just until eggs are incorporated.

Pour the mixture into the prepared baking dish(es). Use 1⁄2 cup per small dish.

Bake for 18-20 minutes for the individual ramekins OR 25-30 minutes for the large baking dish, until the flan is puffed and just set. It should be a golden orange color. Remove and let cool completely.

Refrigerate overnight or at least 4 hours before serving. Serve topped with your favorite ingredients.

STRAWBERRY RHUBARB CRISP

Makes 6-8 servings

4 stalks of rhubarb, chopped
2 pints of strawberries, chopped
3 tablespoons coconut sugar
juice from ½ lemon (about a tablespoon)
2 tablespoons vanilla pea protein powder
½ teaspoon ground cinnamon
a pinch of sea salt

Alternative Filling:
Substitute 3 cups of any fruit combination for the strawberry and rhubarb:
Strawberries; Apples + berries; Apples + banana; Pears; Pineapple + banana

I love this light crisp for dessert, but there's nothing wrong with enjoying it for breakfast. Try adding an extra scoop of protein powder – this sweet treat hides it really well. Make it even more decadent by topping it with a dollop of coconut yogurt. You really can't go wrong with this. I've even given you some easy substitutes if you want to try other fruits. Fast and easy for a dessert, it's good hot, cold, or room temperature. A low-sugar, high protein, totally versatile dessert? I'll take it anyway, any time, any day.

Preheat the oven to 375 degrees.

Mix the rhubarb, strawberries, lemon juice, coconut sugar, protein powder, cinnamon, and salt together until well combined. Bake in a casserole pan for 10 minutes.

While the fruit is in the oven, mix all the crumble ingredients together in a bowl with a spoon. When the fruit casserole comes out after 10 minutes, sprinkle the mixture evenly over the fruit, and bake for another 25 minutes. Let cool before enjoying.

CRISP TOPPING

1 ½ cups almond flour
6 tablespoons coconut flour
6 tablespoons coconut oil
6 tablespoons maple syrup
¾ cup almonds, finely chopped
½ cup walnuts, finely chopped
¼ teaspoon sea salt

CACAO BRAZIL NUT TRUFFLES

Makes 32 truffles

This is my mom's favorite dessert, and I always think of her when I make it. I carry these truffles around for a treat, freeze them for later, and even ship them to my mom in Atlanta. Chocoholics rejoice: these truffles give you all the benefits that raw cacao has to offer.

¹/₃ cup chopped, dry cacao butter (or 1 ounce weighed)
¾ cup melted coconut butter
3 tablespoons melted coconut oil
½ cup cacao powder
½ cup cacao nibs

¼ cup maple syrup
2 teaspoons maca powder
¼ teaspoon finely ground sea salt
2 cups mini semi-sweet chocolate chips (I like Hu chocolate chunks, made with coconut sugar.)

Place the cacao butter, coconut butter, and coconut oil in a double boiler, or in a bowl over a pot of simmering water, without letting the bottom of the bowl touch the water. Stir the contents of the bowl occasionally, until completely melted.

Pour the melted mixture into a food processor, then add the cacao powder, maple syrup, maca powder, cacao nibs, and sea salt. Process for 60 seconds, until the mixture is uniform and resembles a thick paste. Add the chocolate chips and process for just 10 seconds to leave a little crunch in your truffles, or 30-45 seconds if you prefer your truffles smooth.

Pour the mixture into a bowl, and refrigerate, covered, for 40 minutes.

After 40 minutes, remove the bowl from the fridge, and scoop one rounded tablespoon of the mixture onto a baking sheet. Repeat with the rest of the mixture. (You should have roughly 32 scoops.)

Roll each scoop into a firm ball using your hands. If the mixture becomes too soft, refrigerate for another 30 minutes.

Keep the truffles refrigerated, removing them from the fridge 20-30 minutes before serving.

VANILLA PUDDING

Makes 4-6 servings

This is a great sugar-free, high-protein pudding you can enjoy as a breakfast parfait, a dessert, or a snack. I portion it out into small mason jars and keep it in the fridge for an easy snack later..

3 cups coconut milk
3 ripe medium-sized bananas (about 1 ½ cups mashed)
¼ cup vanilla pea protein powder
¼ cup coconut oil
1 tablespoon plus 1 teaspoon grass-fed gelatin powder
1 tablespoon vanilla extract
a pinch of sea salt

Optional toppings: toasted nuts, cacao nibs, unsweetened shredded coconut, fresh berries, buckwheat granola (p. 36), seasonal chia seed compote (p. 45)

Heat 1 cup of the coconut milk in a small pot over medium heat until warmed through.

Measure out the gelatin into a small bowl and set it aside.

Combine the rest of the ingredients (including the rest of the coconut milk) into a blender and blend until smooth.

Whisk the gelatin into the warm coconut milk until dissolved, and then add it into the blender and blend for another 20-30 seconds until very creamy.

Divide the mixture into 8 individual 6-ounce cups or ramekins. Chill for 4 hours or overnight. Add your favorite toppings and serve.

BANANA ICE CREAM
WITH ALMOND BUTTER AND TAHINI CRUMBLE

Makes 2-3 servings

This is a great healthy substitute for store-bought ice cream. I started making it for my nephews, and they don't even miss regular ice cream. If you want it sweeter, just add maple syrup or honey to your liking.

4 medium-sized bananas, peeled and frozen overnight
½ cup unsweetened almond butter plus more for topping (p. 97)
¼ cup almond milk (more if needed)
½ teaspoon cinnamon
a pinch of sea salt
Black Tahini Crumble (p. 31) for topping

Combine the frozen bananas, almond butter, and almond milk in a high-speed blender. Blend, slowly at first, until smooth, adding a bit more almond milk as needed to reach your desired texture.

Once smooth, scoop into a container, cover tightly, and freeze for at least 2 hours for a hard ice cream, or serve immediately as "soft serve."
Top with almond butter and black tahini crumble.

This section is filled with my favorite pestos, sauces, and dips. The little extras are what make your table special. I love to have a big board with lots of dips, veggies, pickles, crackers, and almond cheese for snacking when friends come over. I hope you enjoy some of my favorites.

aiolis, dips, pestos & hummus

AIOLIS

Each recipe makes 2 cups

I love traditional aioli, but when I went through an egg-free phase, I had to create some alternatives. I love having a clean, plant-based creamy aioli to work with. You can make any aioli by adding turmeric, curry, cayenne, or any spice or seasoning that excites you.

MARCONA ALMOND AIOLI

1/3 cup apple cider vinegar
1 tablespoon plus 1 teaspoon honey
¾ cup extra virgin olive oil
¼ cup plus 2 tablespoons finely chopped marcona almonds
¼ teaspoon sea salt

Combine the vinegar and honey in a blender, and slowly drizzle the olive oil in with the blender is still running. Stop the blender and scrape down the sides.

Run the blender again and slowly add the almonds and salt. Continue blending until smooth and creamy, at least a full minute. Store refrigerated in an airtight container.

COCONUT AIOLI

½ cup coconut butter
½ cup extra virgin olive oil
½ cup water
¼ teaspoon sea salt
1 teaspoon chopped garlic

Optional Additions:
¼ cup chopped cilantro and parsley leaves
¼ teaspoon ground black pepper
½ teaspoon sumac

Blend all the ingredients together in a high-speed blender with a tamper until creamy.

AMBER'S CLASSIC EGG AIOLI

1 ¼ cup olive oil
5 egg yolks
½ cup plus 2 tablespoons avocado oil
2 ½ tablespoons lemon juice
1 garlic clove, diced
½ teaspoon sea salt
¼ teaspoon ground black pepper

Combine the egg yolks and the lemon juice in a food processor and pulse until blended.

Mix the 2 oils together, and add them, very slowly, to the running food processor. If you add the oil too fast, it will break the egg yolk and ruin the texture. When the aioli starts to thicken, add the garlic, salt, and pepper.

PESTOS

Each recipe makes 2 cups

I like to think outside the box when it comes to pesto. All you need to make a good pesto is a leafy green or herb, a nut or seed, some olive oil, citrus juice, and the right seasoning. See which combination you like the best, or try something new that's all yours. Now that you know how, you can use whatever you have in the fridge to make an original pesto. I like to use spinach, kale, or arugula if it needs to get used quickly. You can always double a recipe to keep extra in the fridge. Use as a dip, with a cheese board, whisked into a salad dressing, or on top of your favorite meat or fish. Bonus: pestos freeze and thaw easily.

PISTACHIO PESTO

Combining the pistachios with the fresh herbs creates a unique flavor I just love. The fact that pistachios are high in antioxidants and help maintain healthy cholesterol and blood sugar levels makes me happy, too.

1 bunch of cilantro, chopped
1 bunch of parsley, chopped
1 cup activated pistachios
¾ cup olive oil
½ cup torn basil leaves
juice from 2 oranges (about 6 tablespoons)
1 tablespoon fresh ginger root, peeled and chopped
2 cloves garlic
1 teaspoon sea salt
½ teaspoon cumin
¼ teaspoon crushed red pepper flakes

Combine all the ingredients in a food processor and blend until smooth, about 2 minutes.

PARSLEY ALMOND PESTO

I love any way I can sneak more parsley into my diet because of its many health benefits. The slight sweetness of the almonds combined with earthy parsley makes for great flavor.

2 ½ cups parsley leaves, packed, without stems
½ cup almonds
½ cup extra virgin olive oil
12 mint leaves
juice from 1 orange (about 3 tablespoons)
1 clove of garlic
½ teaspoon sea salt
¼ teaspoon ground black pepper

Combine all the ingredients in a food processor and blend until smooth, about 2 minutes.

PUMPKIN SEED CARROT TOP PESTO

I always ask for extra carrot tops at the store or farmer's market. They're the leafy part that is usually cut off by the time you get the carrots. I hate seeing them go to waste since they have plenty of nutritional value. I juice them, use them in broths, salads, and in this delicious pesto that also boasts pumpkin seeds in place of nuts.

2 cups basil
½ cup plus 2 tablespoons extra virgin olive oil
the tops (leaves only) from 1 bunch of carrots, chopped
1 clove garlic
¾ cup activated pumpkin seeds
¼ cup sliced almonds
juice from 1 orange (about 3 tablespoons)
1 tablespoon lemon juice
½ teaspoon sea salt
¼ teaspoon ground black pepper

Combine all the ingredients in a food processor and blend until smooth, about 2 minutes.

ARUGULA PECAN PESTO

I really love bitter greens, and this arugula pesto does fall into the bitter category. But the sweetness of the pecans balances it perfectly, making this a great pesto to dress up grilled fish or veggies.

2 cups arugula
1 cup activated pecans
¾ cups extra virgin olive oil
juice from ½ lemon (about a tablespoon)
1 clove of garlic
1 teaspoon sea salt
½ teaspoon sumac
½ teaspoon paprika
¼ teaspoon crushed red pepper flakes

Combine all the ingredients in a food processor and blend until smooth, about 2 minutes.

FERMENTED VEGGIES

Makes one 64-ounce jar

Eating fermented veggies is known to help increase probiotics and good bacteria in the gut. These are easy to make and always great to have on hand to dress up a salad or wrap, as a side dish or healthy snack.

2 cups green cabbage, sliced (save a few whole cabbage leaves)
2 cups carrots, sliced
1 bunch dandelion greens, chopped
3 tablespoons fresh ginger root, sliced
12 cloves garlic, sliced
¼ teaspoon sea salt
½ bunch of celery, chopped
with 2 cups water

Combine all of the ingredients except the celery and water in a large bowl. Then blend the celery and water in a blender until smooth, and pour the celery juice into the bowl to coat the veggies.

Then pack the veggies and celery juice into a clean glass jar (or a few smaller jars) and top with cabbage leaves. Leave out for up to a week to ferment in the kitchen. Best if the temperature is around 70 degrees. If the kitchen is too cold, you can put it on top of the oven while the oven is on low.

DIPS

Each recipe makes 2-3 cups

ALMOND RICOTTA

2 cups peeled almonds, soaked for
at least 6 hours then strained
¾ cup filtered water
3 tablespoons lemon juice
1 teaspoon sea salt

I buy peeled almonds rather
than do the labor-intensive job
of blanching and peeling them
myself.

Combine the almonds with the rest
of the ingredients in a high-speed
blender and blend until creamy.

CASHEW CREAM

2 cups cashews, soaked for at least
6 hours and strained and strained
¼ cup nutritional yeast
¼ cup water
2 tablespoons lemon juice
2 small cloves of garlic
1 teaspoon sea salt
½ teaspoon ground black pepper

Combine all the ingredients in a
food processor and blend until
smooth, about 2 minutes.

RED PEPPER CASHEW
CREAM

2 cups raw cashews, soaked for at
least 6 hours, and strained
1 red pepper, roasted (about ½
cup)
2 tablespoons lemon juice
2 small cloves garlic
¼ cup nutritional yeast
¼ cup water
1 teaspoon sea salt
1 teaspoon ground black pepper

Roast the red pepper whole on
a baking sheet in a 400-degree
oven for 30 minutes. Then put the
pepper into a small bowl and cover
with plastic wrap or a dishtowel.

When the pepper is cool enough
to handle, peel the charred skin
from the pepper. Cut in half, cut
out the seeds, and discard the top.
Alternatively, you can use ½ cup of
store-bought roasted red pepper.

Combine all the ingredients in a
food processor and blend until
smooth, about 2 minutes.

HUMMUS

Each recipe makes 3 cups

I like to experiment with using different vegetables and using nuts instead of beans for a non-traditional hummus. They are great as a dip, in a wrap, in the soccas (p. 75), or in an endive boat topped with avocado, sunflower seeds, and a drizzle of olive oil.

ROASTED BEET & WALNUT HUMMUS

1 pound red beets, roasted and peeled (3 medium-sized beets)
2/3 cup raw walnuts, soaked and strained
1/3 cup extra virgin olive oil
3 tablespoons tahini
2 tablespoons lemon juice
2 teaspoons red wine vinegar
1 teaspoon sea salt
½ teaspoon chopped garlic
½ teaspoon ground black pepper
¼ teaspoon cumin

Combine all the ingredients in a food processor and blend until smooth, about 2 minutes.

BLACK BEAN HUMMUS

2 cups cooked black beans
1 cup cooked garbanzo beans
2 tablespoons lemon juice
2 tablespoons extra virgin olive oil
1 tablespoon tahini
1 tablespoon minced garlic
1 ½ teaspoons cumin
1 teaspoon sea salt
½ teaspoon cayenne pepper
¼ teaspoon ground black pepper
6 tablespoons water, plus more as needed

Rinse and drain all the beans very well. Then combine all the ingredients except the water in a food processor, blending until very smooth. Slowly add the water while blending to achieve the consistency you like.

YAM HUMMUS

I can't get enough of this bean-free hummus. Use it as a dip, on the oat seed bread (p. 47), cheesy almond crackers (p. 84), wraps, or sandwiches.

2 medium yams, roasted and peeled
½ cup toasted tahini
¼ cup extra virgin olive oil
1 tablespoon red wine vinegar
2 teaspoons cumin
1 teaspoon sea salt
1 teaspoon paprika
½ teaspoon ground black pepper

Combine all the ingredients in a food processor and blend until smooth, about 2 minutes.

what I love about my favorite superfoods

Apple Cider Vinegar	Regulates pH balance in my body, supports detox process, helps to lower my cholesterol, supports my immune system.
Ashwagandha	Great for my body and brain, my mental clarity, my cortisol levels, helps me fight anxiety and depression.
Avocado	Brain food that also supports the health of my eyes and liver, a good source of vitamin K. A healthy fat that satiates me, helping with weight loss and lowering my cholesterol.
Beets	Great source of iron and folic acid. Helps with colon cleansing, blood cleansing. Good for gallbladder and liver, and supports detoxing.
Blue Majik	An extract of spirulina that's anti-inflammatory and supports gut health. Antioxidant, helps relieve physical discomfort, and great for joints, flexibility, and inflammation after exercise. Gives me energy and vitality. Flavorless and beautiful color.
Brazil Nuts	Good source of selenium, great for thyroid health.
Cacao	An antioxidant that gives me energy and a mood lift without spiking my nervous system. Increases dopamine secretion.
Carrots	Support skin, eye, and teeth health, as well as digestion and liver function.
Cauliflower	Contains an enzyme that inhibits cancer and tumor growth. Supports my cardiovascular health, helps me fight inflammation. High in fiber, helping with digestion. Supports bone health.
Chaga	Fights chronic inflammation, fights cancer, supports the immune system, reduces inflammation and oxidative stress, packed with antioxidants.
Chia Seeds	Plant-based protein that's high in fiber, calcium, and omega-3 fatty acids.
Chlorella	An antioxidant that helps supports my skin health, lower my cholesterol, and boost my immune system. High in protein, nutrients, and B vitamins. I feel like I'm glowing when I eat chlorella. It also helps cleanse heavy metals from my body.
Cilantro	Anti-bacterial, anti-fungal, and helps to cleanse toxic metals from my body.
Cinnamon	Helps regulate my blood sugar, assists in weight loss, cholesterol, and circulation. Also great for fighting a cold.
Coconut Oil, Butter	Helps to lower my cholesterol, supports digestion, immune system, brain function, blood sugar, cholesterol, helps fight candida and skin aging.
Collagen	Supports the health of my nails, hair, skin, and bones. High in protein and supports gut health and strong joints. Flavorless.
Dandelion Greens	A favorite food when I'm detoxing or cleansing. Helps support liver detox, balance blood sugar, provides calcium and iron.

Dulse	A seaweed that helps cleanse heavy metals from the body, and is high in iodine, vitamins, and minerals, especially B vitamins, iron, and potassium. Great for thyroid function and a healthy liver.
Flax Meal	High in fiber and omega-3 fatty acids, anti-viral and anti-bacterial, helps lower cholesterol.
Fennel	Supports cardiovascular health, helps fight bad breath. Great for digestion.
Garlic	Antifungal, provides immune system support, healthy cholesterol, and blood sugar levels.
Ginger	Helps me reduce inflammation, supports my immune system and digestion.
Hemp Seeds	Technically a nut, not a seed. A complete protein, they contain all nine essential amino acids. More easily digestible than other nuts, seeds, and grains. Good for my heart, circulation, energy, and help to reduce inflammation.
Lemon Juice	Helps create an alkaline environment in my body, fights flu, cold, and fever. An antioxidant that helps reduce the risk of cancer. Helpful for indigestion, constipation, and energy. It helps flush the liver and kidneys. It has antioxidant, and anti cancer properties.
Lion's Mane	Gives me physical energy, supports brain function and helps with anxiety and depression.
Lucuma	Naturally low-glycemic, gastrointestinal-friendly sweetener. A sugar substitute that's high in antioxidants, vitamins, and minerals.
Maca	Gives me an energy boost, helps increase my physical strength, balances my hormones, and can increase libido. Not recommended for people who are pregnant or breastfeeding.
Matcha	Gives me energy without jitters, high in antioxidants, helps boost metabolism, supports a healthy immune system.
MCT Oil	Gives sustained energy and mental focus; helps regulate appetite and burn fat.
Mesquite	Great for hair and skin, helps balance sugar levels, a good source of magnesium.
Monk Fruit	A low-glycemic sugar substitute. Sweet without the sugar crash.
Mustard Seed Powder	Helps my body absorb the nutrients from cruciferous vegetables.
Nutritional Yeast	Vegan-friendly cheese flavor that's high in fiber, protein, vitamin B12, and iron and provides 18 amino acids. An inactive yeast.
Parsley	Helps digestive health, high in iron, antioxidants, and nutrients that support eye health. Contains vitamin B folate which may reduce the risk of heart disease.
Psyllium Husk	High in fiber, aids digestion, and helps reduce blood sugar.
Pumpkin Seeds	Contain tryptophan, which helps produce serotonin, and melatonin which promote healthy sleep. Good for metabolism, high in protein, magnesium, zinc, healthy fats, antioxidants, and fiber
Purple Sweet Potato	Very high in antioxidants. Sweet potatoes are my favorite carb.
Reishi	Supports a healthy immune system and brain, promotes longevity, and helps prevent premature aging.
Sea Salt	Contains more than 80 minerals, helps control water levels in my body, helps to balance electrolytes, and increases absorption of nutrients.
Sunflower Seeds	A good source of antioxidants; supports healthy bones.
Tahini	High in calcium, magnesium, and potassium. Aids liver detox.
Tocos	Great skin food - the best source of bioavailable vitamin E.
Turmeric	Fights and prevents inflammation. A big support when I was recovering from surgery. Anti-fungal, anti-viral, natural pain-killer, helps wounds heal faster, supports a healthy immune system, fights premature aging.
Yams	High in vitamin B6, aids in digestion and high fiber helps regulate bowels.

acknowledgements

What a journey this project has been. This book has been in the works for over 3 years, but it really came to life in 2019 when I partnered with Lizzie Rose to reimagine, write, and finish this book in divine timing. I am so blessed by how gracefully this has all come together with the help of my team, and the support of my family and friends. So much dedication, passion, energy, love, creativity, time, and patience went into creating this book, and I am grateful that this book will bring some light, nourishment, and health to all who use it. I could not have done it alone. I am so grateful to:

Magical Lizzie Rose, a soul sister, and my co-author. Her passion, intuition, creativity, and brilliance with putting it all together made this all possible.

The creative photography and art direction team, Jake and Hailee Repko. Their beautiful pictures capture my passion for food and bring this book to life.

Stacie Martinez, the creative, talented, and enthusiastic graphic designer who assembled this book through its many phases.

Reyna Pecot, my talented sous chef, who tested, tasted, and perfected these recipes with me.

Chef Nikki, for her amazing palate and for testing and tasting the recipes with us.

Keghan Hurst for her eye and hand to bring this book in sync with my brand and my heart's message.

Donna and Suzy Pruden, the publishers of this book, for bringing it to the shelves and believing in me.

My amazing parents and sister who have always been by my side as my biggest supporters in all that I do. (And for tasting hundreds of recipes over the years.)

My Source Cafe family for always supporting me and joining me on my mission in life.

index

A

adaptogen 13, 15, 18–19, 23, 29, 97–98
    cacao latte, 18
aioli 43, 77, 90, 105
    amber's classic egg aioli, 105
    coconut aioli, 43, 77, 90, 105
    egg aioli, 43, 90, 105
    marcona almond aioli, 105
almond butter, 16, 26, 36, 40–41, 97, 102
    butter syrup, 40–41, 46
    crumble, 72
    date milk, 16, 31
    flour, 45–46, 78, 94, 96, 100
    milk, 20, 78, 102
    ricotta, 70, 72, 75, 108
almond butter, organic creamy, 16
apple cider vinegar, 20, 45–46, 48, 90, 105, 110
arugula pecan pesto, 35, 107
ashwagandha, 15, 18, 98, 110
avocado, 11–12, 23–26, 29, 35, 39–40, 46–47, 53–58,
    61–62, 75–76, 79, 82, 87–90, 105, 109–110
avocado cashew toast, 35
avocado oil, 11–12, 39–40, 62, 76, 79, 82, 87–90, 105

B

banana, 24–26, 29, 34, 36, 38, 40, 49, 94, 100, 102
    banana chocolate chip muffins, 49
    banana ice cream with almond butter and tahini
    crumble, 102
bananza, 26
beet puree, 48
beets, 24, 48, 66, 109–110
berry chia seed compote, 45
bison bolognese with zucchini noodles, 91
bison burger, 90

bison, wild, 11, 71, 81, 88, 90–91
black bean hummus, 75, 109
blenders, 23
blue majik, 96, 110
blue majik power balls, 96
brain fuel latte, 19
brazil nuts, 16, 25, 37, 110
broccoli rice, 79, 88
browned rice, pesto, veggies, 76
brussels sprout salad, 64
buckwheat bread, 35, 45–46, 58
    granola, 15, 29, 34, 36, 102
    groats, 36, 47
butternut squash, kale, onions, seeds & herbs, 71

C

cacao
    almond butter cup, 26
    brazil nut truffles, 101
    nibs, 25, 34, 95, 99, 101–102
    powder, 15–16, 18, 26, 31, 34, 98, 101
    cacao butter, 101
carrots, 12, 24, 53, 58, 61, 63, 76, 91, 107, 110
cashew cream, 35, 39, 55–56, 58, 63, 65, 72–73, 84, 108
cauliflower
    cacao peppermint bowl, 31
    coconut soup, 56
    oatmeal, 38
cayenne pepper, 20, 109
chaga, 110
cheesy almond crackers, 84, 109
chestnut cream soup, 57
chlorella, 12, 29, 53, 110
chopped mint, 65
cilantro, 12, 25, 35, 58, 62, 64, 71, 75, 79, 88, 105–106, 110
cinnamon coconut pecans, 29, 35, 37, 40–41
coconut
    aioli, 43, 77, 90, 105
    flour, 46
    hollandaise sauce, 43
    milk, 12, 17, 26, 29, 38–40, 48, 53–57, 73, 79, 99, 102
    water, 25, 29, 36
    cream, whipped, 99
    unsweetened shredded, 25, 36–38, 41, 94–95,
    99, 102
cod, 12, 70, 86, 89
creamy kelp noodle salad, 63

D

dandelion greens, 25, 58, 88, 107, 110
deboning fish, 89
dulse, 23, 29, 58, 79, 88, 111

E

everyone's favorite bison sauté, 88

F

fast nut milk, 16
fennel bulb, 54–55, 58, 71, 75
fermented veggies, 43, 107
flax meal, 36–37, 40, 46, 96, 111
frisée, 43
frittata, 39
frozen
    fruits, 24
    raw zucchini, 29
    veggies, 24

G

gluten-free
    flour, 12, 40, 48–49, 51
    oat, 36, 47, 97
granulated monk fruit sweetener, 12, 15, 31, 41, 48–49, 51, 95
green goddess bowl, 29
green smoothie, 25
green soup, 53

H

healing broth, 58
hemp seed coconut milk, 17, 26, 29, 38, 40 hemp seeds, 17, 25, 29, 45, 73, 97, 111
homemade almond butter, 97
hummus, roasted beet & walnut, 109

J

job's tears, 82

K

kabocha, 39, 54
kabocha squash coconut cream soup, 54
kale salad, 65–66

L

latte, 16, 18–20
    adaptogen cacao, 18
    matcha, 19
    turmeric, 20
lentil curry stew, 58
lion's mane mushroom, 12, 18
lucuma powder, 18, 29, 31, 37

M

maca, 12–13, 15, 18–19, 23, 26, 29, 31, 97–98, 101, 111
maple syrup, 11, 15–16, 18–20, 26, 31, 34–38, 41, 45, 94, 97, 100–102
maple tahini sweet potato toast, 34
matcha powder, 19, 26, 96
matcha smoothie, 26
melted coconut butter, 101
mesquite powder, 18, 31
monk fruit
    powder, 12, 24, 96, 98
    sweetener, 12, 15, 31, 48–49, 51, 95
mushroom marinade, 63
mustard seed powder, 78–79, 111

N

nut & seed milks, 15
nut butters, 23

O

oat blueberry bites, 97
oat seed bread, 35, 43, 47, 55, 109
onion, 53–56, 58, 63, 71, 78–79, 88–91
    cashew cream, 63
overnight banana oatmeal, 36

P

paleo granola bar, 94
paleo porridge, 37

paleo protein snack bread, 46
parsley almond pesto, 106
parsnip and sweet potato gratin, 78
pecans, toasted, 55, 99
persimmon, 35
pistachio & cashew cream toast, 35
pistachio pesto, 46, 64, 106
polenta, 73
protein pancakes, 40
protein powders, 23–24
psyllium husk, 38, 45, 47, 111
pudding, vanilla, 102
pumpkin
    bread, 51
    puree, 51, 95
pumpkin seed
    carrot top pesto, 70, 76, 90, 107
    seed cinnamon milk, 17, 19
purple smoothie bowl, 29
purple sweet potato, 29, 31, 34, 111

Q

quinoa, 12, 60, 65
quinoa & kale salad, 65

R

radicchio, 65–66
raw carrot beet salad, 61
red cashew & pesto toast, 35
red pepper cashew, 35, 58, 72–73, 108
red pepper cashew cream, 35, 58, 72–73, 108
refueler yam smoothie, 25
reishi mushroom powder, 18

S

salmon dip with almond aioli, 84
salmon, seared, 70, 82
sautéed apples, 99
sea bass with salsa verde, 87
semi-sweet chocolate, 101
sherry vinegar, 63, 66, 76, 84, 88, 90
simple green salad, 58, 60–61, 70, 88
simple matcha latte, 19
smoked salmon benedict, 43

soccas, 75
    mediterranean style, 75
    mexican style, 75
spaghetti squash casserole, 72
steamed cod with herbed cauliflower rice, 86
stone fruit salad, 62
strawberry rhubarb crisp, 100
sumac, 35, 39, 56–57, 63, 78–79, 84, 87, 90, 105, 107
sweet potatoes, 24, 29, 111

T

tahini, 23, 31, 34, 66, 76, 98, 102, 109, 111
    black tahini crumble, 31, 34, 102
    maple tahini sweet potato toast, 34
    orange tahini dressing, 76
    roasted carrots, 76
    zucchini brownies with tahini frosting, 98
tocos powder, 18–19, 29, 31
tri-nut milk, 16
tuscan kale, 65–66, 71, 82, 88–89

V

vanilla pudding, 102

W

walnuts, activated, 16, 37

X

xanthan gum, 48–49, 51

Y

yam, 24-45, 55, 77, 99, 109, 111
    fennel soup, 55
    fries with coconut aioli, 77
    hummus, 109

Z

zucchini brownies with tahini frosting, 98
zucchini noodles, 70–71, 91

Share your stories and connect with Chef Amber online for more health and wellness insights.

🌐 Explore new recipes and cooking classes at chefamber.com

📷 Share your creations and tell us your favorite's from the book! @chefamberla #chefamberla

120